The
eBay®
Revolution

*How Brilliant
Entrepreneurs
are Cashing in
on eBay...*

Their Individual Stories

Bill Bishop

LEGEND PUBLISHING

Published by:
Legend Publishing
P.O. Box 131571
Carlsbad, CA 92013
800-818-0101
www.netlegends.net

Legend Publishing books are available at special quantity discounts to use as premiums and sales promotions, or for use in training and educational programs. For more information, please contact Legend Publishing.

ISBN 0-9762572-0-3

Printed in the United States of America

To the entrepreneurial spirit in all of us

Acknowledgements

I am grateful to the people whom I interviewed for this book: Chuck Black, Bill Cameta, Brandon Dupsky, Rich Horowitz, Mike Levinson, Ray Lindstrom, Martin Mathews, Karen McMasters, Johnny Morgan, Mike Ray, Ravi Sambhwani, Mike Wuertz, Rob Yeremian, and Karen Young. I appreciate their time and effort, and I look forward to lifelong relationships with them. This venture allowed me to meet special people whom I otherwise would never have had the opportunity to know.

Thank you, Jianda Johnson, for your encouragement and assistance. You are special and I look forward to seeing your talents blossom, as I am sure they will.

Ingrid Bremner, I so much enjoyed working with you. You came along at the right time. I felt close even though you were on the opposite coast.

Diane Thompson, you went the extra mile as you always do. When you returned from your mission to Kenya it was a pleasure to include you in this project. Our friendship over the years has meant a lot to me and it was fun working with you. Your expertise and experience made a positive difference.

Craig Beery, you are a remarkable person and have contributed a great deal to this book. Your high energy is always uplifting. You have the rare ability to see things from a micro and macro viewpoint at the same time. I look forward to future endeavors.

My interest in computers dates back to the late 1960's when, after receiving my MBA from the University of Southern California, I joined IBM as a new account salesman in their data processing division. I have always gravitated toward marketing challenges and worked as an advisor to the marketing departments of Lawry's, Mattel, Avery, E. & J. Gallo Winery, Amtrak and Pentel. Recently I co-authored *We Are All Champions* with Ken Norton, former World Heavyweight Boxing Champion.

When I joined IBM I did not envision anything in my wildest imagination close to what has happened with computers and ultimately with the Internet. In those early days all data was keypunched on 80 column cards before being loaded into computers. Virtually all applications had to be custom programmed. I am sure that in the next 25 years, when we look back at today, we will see an even greater magnitude of technical advancement than what we've seen in the past 25 years.

It is only fitting that I express my thanks and gratitude to all the people interviewed in this book. Their cooperation and honesty is to be commended and is greatly appreciated. None of them asked to be individually promoted. The strong feeling that they projected to me in the interviews was that each one wanted to give rather than receive. Those selected to be included in this book offer valuable information and advice for anyone interested in Internet marketing. They were chosen from among thousands of successful entrepreneurs who market their products on the Internet. There are numerous messages to be heard from these interviews, and I suggest this book could be read more than once and used repeatedly as a reference for getting started on eBay.

Each interview is unique based on the personality and experiences of the entrepreneur, but there are common observations that run throughout. Some of these Internet marketers got started selling single surplus items on eBay;

others came with years and years of retail experience or with a strong business background. The Internet offers a level playing field and promising opportunity for all. It is truly another frontier.

This book is intended to document the experiences and strategies of some of the pioneers of the Internet revolution. It is not intended to promote any one marketing approach, but each of the persons interviewed use eBay as a significant vehicle of their Internet marketing strategy. Most of them create the majority of their Internet sales from eBay.

To predict the future of Internet marketing is like knowing where the needle in the hay stack will be. My gut feeling is that there will be numerous companies competing with eBay. All indications are, if the forecasted growth of Internet marketing takes place, that there will be room for many emerging companies. It is fascinating that eBay grew from humble beginnings in 1995 when founder Pierre Omidyar launched an online auction. This is an indication of how it is possible for a company to develop tremendous growth in a relatively short period of time.

At the end of the book I recap some of the recurrent messages that stood out to me from the interviews. You may find other messages that speak to you as being equally valuable. This book is written in non-technical terms so that most everyone can easily understand its contents. In case certain words and terms are unfamiliar to the reader, a glossary is included for clarification.

Bill Bishop

Contents

||||||||||||||||||||||||||||||||||||||||||||||||||||||||||||

Karen Young

She Found a Need

||||||||||||||||||||||||||||||||||||||||||||||||||||||||||||

If I need it, others need it too. Selling household items she no longer needed progressed into a business. Karen Young soon recognized the need for a source of low cost shipping supplies. She knew if she would benefit from a better source, so would others. Her empathy of other people's needs, along with tenacity, helped her launch a thriving business.

So Karen, tell me how you were first introduced to the Internet?

Years and years ago my father bought a new computer and gave me his old one. My first computer was an old IBM 286. It was very outdated and probably obsolete at the time. It had one megabyte of RAM and didn't even run Windows. I think it only had a ten megabyte hard drive, so I used it to learn how to upgrade computers. The first thing I had to do was to start adding memory and a bigger hard drive, so I could install Windows. I learned to do it all myself, and it founded my love of computers. I started upgrading computers for friends and doing little repairs for friends of friends, and that's how I started my small computer business. After doing repairs and upgrades I moved on to building and selling new computers to friends and family. My first exposure to the Internet was chatting on a local bulletin board. I started needing parts to upgrade the computers I was fixing, so I began looking on the Internet and found auction sites. Although eBay was in existence at the time, it was very small. I used a couple of other auction houses at first, but I eventually moved over to eBay around April of '99 to buy most of my computer parts. I had my first experience selling on eBay a little later. I had boxes of old, obsolete computer software lying around and I listed them for sale. I was totally shocked when I sold them all. So I started going through my garage looking for other stuff to sell. After my mother moved in with us, we took most of what we didn't need after combining our two households, to our local auction guys and sold them. We still had stuff out in the garage that no one was using. I went through it all and selected items to put up for sale on eBay. They did really well. Then I used the proceeds to buy more items at the local auction. I had no idea what I was doing. I didn't know anything about collectibles or antiques. I was just buying whatever items caught my eye, thinking I could sell them for more than what I'd paid. The items sold very well on eBay and they had large profit margins. I took the money from those sales and bought a digital camera. Most people on eBay didn't have pictures in their ads yet. I went back into action and bought more of whatever caught my eye. I listed all these items on eBay, but this time I included pictures. This made a big difference. Then I branched out to different local auctions and estate sales, mainly estate auctions where someone's grandma or grandpa had died and people were auctioning their belongings. Some of these auction businesses allowed me to take certain items on consignment. You can find these types of auctions everywhere.

Did the high cost of your shipping materials and supplies encourage you to find ways to reduce these costs?

I got up to selling around 100 items a week, so I had to hire my first employee to come in and help me package things. Once I had an item photographed and listed, I would just have her box it up for me. It really came to light that I was spending a lot of money on the cost of shipping supplies. I thought there must be a cheaper way to get supplies than from OfficeMax or Wal-Mart. I knew everyone else on eBay was spending too much money on shipping supplies, as well. When I started selling shipping supplies and ordering large quantities, they overran my house and within a month I had to rent a warehouse. I started getting truckloads of bubble wrap in, and boom! I had a bubble wrap shipping supply business. I phased out of buying items from auctions and estate sales to resell on eBay. I've still got a mountain of items that I never got around to selling years ago! [Laughs.] I was telling my husband we need to have a yard sale this summer. We could advertise our yard sale as a "Going out of eBay Business Sale!" [Laughs.]

You changed your eBay User ID to "shippingsupply.com". Was that done so people could relate more to your focus on shipping supplies?

Yes. It better represented our focus to provide a source for shipping supplies.

Have you always managed the business by yourself?

Yes, and the business has always been fun. In the early days, I hired my dad and he wrote all the programs to run my business. Back then there was no such thing as auction management software or PayPal. I had to quickly get a merchant account so that I could take credit cards. I was getting tons of credit card payments a day. I had to manually type in every credit card order. It was a real pain so I hired my dad. The first program he wrote for me was designed to help me automate the processing of credit card orders.

How did your father become computer literate?

As a young man he worked for White Motor Company, when IBM was just coming out with computer systems for businesses. White Motor Company decided they wanted to get their trucking company hooked up with computers and they needed to send someone to IBM's training center to learn computer systems and programming. They chose my dad and once he got White Motor Company going, he was in demand nationwide. He was one of the few people that knew what was going on in the early days of business computers. That was a long time ago. He passed down his old computers to my brother and me and that's how I ended up with my first computer.

Do you remember what year IBM trained your dad?

We moved to Georgia in 1966, so it would have probably been 1963 when my dad did his IBM training. I remember the days as a small child, going out to work with him and all those machines with the big tapes spinning around—the computers filled up room after room. They were huge. I guess my interest goes all the way back to childhood. I've got three brothers and one sister, and two of my brothers are in computers in some way or another. So my dad passed it on.

If you're going to be successful on eBay, you have to put customer service up there as a top priority.

That's how the chain reaction started!

Yes.

eBay offers a number of options. Let's cover some of them and the reasoning behind your choices.

Okay. Sure

How many days do you usually run your auctions and how do you determine this?

It depends, but usually I choose three day listings. I also run a few ten day featured category listings. It costs the same to run a three, five or seven day listing. Running a listing for ten days costs an extra twenty cents. One of the eBay rules is that at any given point in time you can list the same item for sale in no more than ten separate listings. If I want to sell more than one bag of peanuts, I can have ten bags in ten different listings. I cannot have more than that. The sooner you cycle it out, say over three days, the sooner you can get it back up there. That is the advantage of a shorter listing. Another kind of listing you can use on eBay is a Dutch auction. I use those all the time. Dutch auctions offer one item, but with multiple quantities of this item in one listing. With a Dutch auction, if there are 150 rolls of bubble wrap in one listing your customer can buy anywhere from 1 to 150 rolls.

Does eBay charge you more for a Dutch auction?

Yes and no. Your insertion fee is based on the initial price of the item. If I were selling a three dollar item, my listing fee would be thirty-five cents. If I'm selling 100 three-dollar items in that same listing, it costs me a little bit more, but it actually costs less per item. You need to calculate an optimum quantity to list in order to take advantage of certain price breaks.

I noticed you have a 99.9% positive feedback rating. That's incredible!

If you're going to be successful on eBay, you have to put customer service up there as a top priority. When I first started selling shipping supplies there was only one other person who was doing what I was doing, although not to the same extent that I was doing it. He was offering limited items. I was the first one who was only selling shipping supplies and I had a more expanded inventory. In the years since, everybody's jumped on the bandwagon and the competition is incredible. The one thing you can do to distinguish yourself from your competition is to offer good customer service. It is important to answer your emails as quickly as you can. Don't let them sit there for days. Always return your phone calls and email your customers to let them know their order has been shipped and give them their tracking number. You have to go that extra distance.

When we last talked your computer had gone down and you needed to send out emails letting people know their items had been shipped. Were you able to get back to those people on a timely basis?

I didn't really run into that many problems. The problem I had was not knowing what my PayPal receipts were. I get an email notice when payments have been received. Since my email was down, I wasn't getting these notices. I had to go to my PayPal account and look up every single individual purchase and payment to find the details including the addresses. I had to print them out and enter them all manually rather than being able to bulk process them using the program my father had written. My dad went far beyond writing the programming that enabled us to process credit card orders. He also wrote all my inventory management software. He may have been the original auction management programmer! We talked about marketing his software, but we decided we're just not in that business. It never would have panned out. Now there are companies that are associated with eBay and they have access to information we never had. Unfortunately my dad passed away last fall. I've had a lot of help setting up this business from my family. My original website was designed by my brother, and my dad did the programming. My mother is currently my customer service representative. She handles the phones for me. My husband quit his job and worked with me for a while, but he's recently gone back into the workforce. He still works here some. He does payroll and a lot of my accounting.

What kind of advice do you have for someone who wants to develop a part-time or full-time Internet business?

Anybody can do what I did. Anybody can go to an auction or garage sale and buy something for ten dollars and then offer it on eBay for twenty dollars. Honestly representing what you are selling is very important. When you're describing the items that you're selling, you have to be honest in your description and mention any flaws the item has. You have to remember these folks are buying something from you that they've only seen in a two dimensional picture. With your words you have to give them a vision for seeing a three dimensional object. The better job you can do with that, the better your sales are going to be. I learned when I was sixteen and got my first job at McDonald's that the customer is always right. Even if you know the customer's completely wrong, "The customer's still always right." I've kept a lot of that philosophy with me as I've grown my business. I always try to treat my customers as I want to be treated. It's helpful for me to think about what I would want a company to do for me in the same situation. That's what I try to do for my customers.

Martin Mathews

A Creative Mind

He shaped wire into his future. Martin Mathews was brought up with an appreciation for antiques. With a creative mind and help from his brother, he crafted replica antique wire products. This was over twenty years ago. Mathews Wire illustrates a classic example of the evolution of a company's marketing strategies – from flea markets, to gift stores, to a company website, and finally eBay.

Your business history goes way back with flea markets and pawnshops. How did that all start?

My family was always into antiques. At an early age I had an unusual understanding of antiques, precious metals and jewelry. I started a manufacturing business right out of high school in 1985 and made country decorating products. Most of them were reproduction antiques. That business did really well. We went from my brother's garage to eventually employing one hundred and thirty-five people. In 1993 our business started to struggle because of changing decorating trends and a lot of pressure from imports. In the last few years there are problems associated with retail stores being overstocked. There is also an uncertain economy since September 11th. eBay has really helped us hold onto our business and pay wages and expenses, and keep us going.

Were you selling antiques when you started the company?

No. We sold wire products. Mainly kitchen gadgets and carpet beaters, and things like that.

Are you still selling to gift stores or are you only selling on eBay?

We sell to gift stores, everything from mom and pop stores to Sears and JC Penny.

How did you get started with your wire products?

At first we used decorative Victorian fence wire. It is really hard to get now, but it was fairly plentiful back when we started, and we made these really fancy carpet beaters, pillow fluffers and little kitchen gadgets. They were just so pretty that they really caught on. That's how we got our start. We bought conventional wire from different sources and started making gadgets and rug beaters. We even made some small furniture and branched out into making wood products and some flat steel products.

Were they replicas that you made?

Yes. We might make them a little fancier than they originally were or we might give them an alternate purpose. For instance, we might make a replica of a set of ice tongs so they can hold paper towels.

How did you first learn about eBay?

I had the idea for an online auction years before I had ever heard of eBay. Of course, eBay already existed, but I wasn't aware of them. Later on I had a girl in the office who was somewhat familiar with eBay. I said, "Hey, sales are faltering. I've got a lot of closeout/discontinued merchandise here." When you run a mail order catalog company, you always have excess inventory from last year's catalog that just sits in the warehouse. We always had a lot of that so we started selling our excess merchandise on eBay and it sold really well. We've now been using eBay about 5 years.

You could've hired Meg Whitman, the CEO of eBay, and started your own online auction business! [Laughs.]

Oh, Yes! [Laughs.]

I've noticed you use a gallery photo on about half of your products.

Yes. I think it's fairly important to use a gallery photo. I determine whether to use a gallery photo by whether or not I'm protecting the item. If I wanted $9.00 for an item and start the bidding at $9.00, then I probably would not use a gallery photo. If I listed the same item but started the bidding at 95 cents, and still wanted $9.00 for it, then I'd probably use a gallery photo to get as much bidding action I could. When you are surfing eBay and you pull up a list of the items that you're searching or a seller's total listing of items, and you look down the left side and see all the little gallery pictures, it makes it more interesting. Auctions without the gallery pictures are more boring. You're less apt to click on those. I think the gallery photo is worth the money.

It looks like just a few of your items have a Buy-It-Now option.

I don't use the Buy-It-Now option often. I've always been involved with the placement of our auctions, and I don't lean toward using Buy-It-Now. I feel neutral about the Buy-It-Now feature. It can be a way to sell more products. I have seen people come into my site and go crazy and buy dozens of items that are listed as a Dutch auction, and also buy up all the Buy-It-Now items we have listed. This is usually when a new buyer sees our auction items for the first time. Like a candle retailer who's never heard of Matthews Wire. They stock up on our items because our prices on eBay are really inexpensive. In most cases they're below wholesale.

How well do Dutch auctions work?

They don't work that well for most people. Someone from eBay commented that we were one of the only sellers who even used the Dutch auction anymore. They were even thinking about getting rid of Dutch auctions altogether. Dutch auctions are invaluable for our business, because they help us sell the products we're trying to closeout. Let's say we we're listing an item that we have thousands of, like little candle holders. If I list them at $9.90 for a dozen that means I would be getting less than a dollar a piece. I can use the Dutch auction instead and list 50 of them at 99 cents each. That works out better for me. Some people come in and say, "Well, you've got 50 sets available. I'll take all 50 sets." Dutch auctions work very well that way.

Reserve prices are bad and really a turnoff to a serious buyer.

Does eBay only charge you for what you sell on Dutch auctions?

Yes. There is a small fee to list and then a normal percentage on what you sell.

Are you using a reserve price?

I hardly ever use a reserve price. Reserve prices are generally not a good way to go. I think eBay should give people who list with no reserve preferential treatment as long as they start the opening bid at 95 cents or less. This would create an incentive for sellers to create a more free market.

The buyer doesn't know until they have placed a bid, as to whether or not an item has a reserve price. Correct?

eBay tells you after you make a bid that the reserve price has not been met, if the bid is less than the reserve price. Before they bid they don't know if there is a reserve. Reserve prices are bad and really a turnoff to a serious buyer. I don't have much good to say about reserve prices except for special circumstances. I have tried to sell a piece of real estate on eBay several times. It is a very valuable piece of real estate worth a half a million dollars. Of course, I don't want to put it on there with no reserve price. In a case like that, I think it is very wise to use a reserve price. People should stick to selling items on eBay when they're willing to let the market set the item's value. I recently opened up an eBay "drop-off" in downtown Frankfort. The eBay User ID for this drop-off business is "whsl1" rather than my regular eBay User ID "mwire." I won't accept anything with a reserve price at my drop-off. Either you want to sell an item on a worldwide auction and accept the price you'll receive in this free market or I don't want to sell it for you. We also use our drop-off eBay User ID to buy things. We have branched out into the eBay drop-off. There aren't any others close to us geographically who have a drop-off, so it looks like it's going to be a good thing for us.

What is the eBay drop-off?

That's where you open a business selling things for other people. We do all the selling, shipping and collecting of the sales proceeds. Then we cut them a check based on the proceeds less our commission. We do it for a 25% commission. We take possession of it. It's like consignment. A guy brought in an entire estate and it'll probably take us close to a year to sell his stuff. He has some really good merchandise, a lot of gold coins. We've also had a lot of positive results selling automobiles. My girlfriend runs an auto detail shop. She started selling cars for us on eBay and so far has sold fifteen cars.

Does she warehouse the cars?

She has a place to keep the cars. The owner signs over the title to her and she sells the car for them. Normally she does a little work on the interior and exterior to make them look as good as possible before she sells them. That business has worked very well for her, even though the eBay fees for selling automobiles are quite high. We keep the Matthews Wire businesses separate from the eBay drop-off business. My brother is not a partner in the eBay drop-off. He retired from working at the business full time this year, but he still works a few days a week. We are going through a transition period.

I can see the potential of the eBay drop-off concept. If you've never sold anything on eBay, you might be better off letting someone else list and sell your items for you.

Yes and getting started can be mind-boggling. It seems simple to somebody who's been doing it for a while, but if you're not familiar with eBay, it can really be pretty overwhelming.

Are you using any kind of an auction management service?

No. I wish I could find one that worked well for us but our software at the manufacturing company is customized. We've tried several of the different auction management software programs, but when we try to re-list an item there's so much HTML gibberish that it's really a nightmare.

How do you keep track of your inventory?

We normally just print out sheets and decide which items we need to re-list that day or that week. Then we mark them and then have people go through and re-list all the items manually. That's definitely not the quickest or cheapest way to do it, but it's the only way to stay on top of the inventory. Inventory is hard for us to manage and keep track of.

What else causes you problems?

It's very stressful for our employees to deal with some eBay customers. You wouldn't believe some of the emails we get. When we tell someone that we're going to give a refund, we give a refund. We still get nasty emails from people. I've bought stuff on eBay and had a problem with it, and had the sellers promise they are sending me a refund. I've been burned several times and never received the refund. It's surprising how some people fly off the handle for no cause. One of the big down sides of eBay is it can be very stressful.

Have you seen eBay change since you joined five years ago?

Yes and I think they've all been for the better. They really know what they're doing. They have people sitting around just thinking of what to do next. I don't know what we'd do without them. Our business has become very dependent on eBay. I would say about 40 % of our business comes from them. This is pretty good considering five years ago we had no sales being generated from eBay.

Did you have a regular website before joining eBay?

Yes. Probably about two or three years before we started selling on eBay we had a website.

How do you bring traffic into your website?

Well, we don't really use the site for that much. We used to do a lot of trade publication advertising and we would mention our website address in those ads. We mostly focused on using manufacturer representatives nationwide. We still do some advertising. We displayed our products in a showroom at the world trade center in Atlanta. One of our representatives had space there. His rent was a hundred thousand dollars a year; they have all basically gone out of business. Ever since around 1995 there has been a very serious decline in the whole manufacturer representative concept.

So are you still selling to gift stores from your website?

Yes. Our site is almost 100% wholesale business.

Are you doing much in the area of international sales?

We still do a little bit of business with Canada, and a little bit with England and Japan. We used to do a whole lot of business with Japan, but it was not done on eBay.

How about your eBay business?

We don't try to sell overseas, but we sometimes do. It can be more of a pain than it's worth. If you're selling very expensive products it might be a good thing, but we sell very inexpensive products. If somebody pays $30 for something, they don't want to pay $50 for shipping. When you do sell something overseas sometimes you want to grit your teeth because it's a hassle.

Are overseas buyers paying through PayPal?

Yes, normally. Sometimes they'll send an international money order. Items almost always get broken when shipping internationally. I feel bad having to charge them so much for shipping and when an item gets broken they want their money back. We have to wait 60 days in some cases to collect insurance. It can be a real pain keeping all that paperwork for up to 90 days.

When you set your website up prior to eBay did it cost a lot of money?

We had a local company printing our catalogs. They were creating websites for small businesses. I got a bare bones website, so it didn't cost very much to set up. The initial cost and all the required maintenance didn't cost very much. We've rebuilt it twice and have had regular updates done at least every three months. We still are probably looking at less than $8000 for everything. Originally it cost about $3,500, so it wasn't costly.

Do you have any feel for where the Internet is headed?

Well, I think that broadband and DSL connections are such an improvement over what we had before. Increased international business may be good for eBay.

Our business has become very dependent on eBay.

Do you think eBay will focus on expanding their foreign presence?

I know that eBay's been aggressively buying services in other countries. They just bought a company in India. The Indian online auction service is big. I hope eBay doesn't become too aggressive. This may cause them unnecessary problems. It's been unfortunate for some companies when they go into a market and don't have adequate knowledge. We import a lot of merchandise from India. They tell you one thing and the next day they're changing their policy. Hopefully eBay has done their research concerning their overseas business ventures.

You personally import from India?

Yes. We've been importing since about 1996. About 20% of our product line is made either in India, Mexico or China. The rest of it we manufacture here.

Do you think you might expand your level of imports?

Not if I can help it. I don't like importing. In the beginning we only imported things that were too difficult for us to make ourselves at a reasonable price. As time went on we got lazy and had a few things made that we actually could build ourselves. Now, with the worldwide steel crunch, our import prices have gone up significantly from China and India. Some of the products we were importing we are now making ourselves here. The steel price increase is another issue that has been hard on us. Our raw materials cost has gone up almost 300 % in the last three years.

Due to the international demand for steel?

Yes. China is buying all the steel that the world can produce and that's not supposed to change. They're building bridges, infrastructure and buildings. I just talked to somebody who was over there and he said it was incredible how much building they are doing. As you can imagine, when steel prices almost triple, it is because of the demand caused by all the building that's going on. It's caused us a lot of problems. The average person still thinks wire is cheap. Well it is about $1.52 a pound right now. Believe me, a pound isn't very much. Three years ago the most we paid was around 72 cents per pound, and sometimes as low as 38 cents per pound. Our wire now runs anywhere from $1.21 to $1.79 per pound. This is an incredible price for steel.

Can anyone start an eBay business and be successful?

Well, I think it's a great opportunity for everyone. A person can go through the learning curve easily by selling items at first that they don't want or need. You basically entice the potential buyer by starting with a low opening bid. The majority of the items we sell are things people don't absolutely need, yet they buy them because they are inexpensive and a good value. eBay is also a great vehicle for closeout sales. As far as we know eBay's the best way to get rid of excess merchandise. You might want to do a little fishing and sell something that you don't necessarily care about and see at what price you can get for it. The first thing a person needs to do is get their eBay positive feedback rating built up so buyers feel comfortable about doing business with them. I think eBay offers an excellent business opportunity. Based on current trends, the timing to start selling on eBay could not be better.

||||||||||||||||||||||||||||||||||||||||||||||||||||||||||||||||||||||

Ray Lindstrom

A Promoter's Promoter

||||||||||||||||||||||||||||||||||||||||||||||||||||||||||||||||||||||

It's in his blood. Ray Lindstrom's experience with marketing and advertising started with radio and television. He is not afraid to aggressively go all out once a test market proves itself. He finds out what works and then expands his promotions full bore. He always sees the big picture. From radio, television, cable and ultimately the Internet, Ray knows how to adjust and still practice the fundamentals he has mastered in communications. Ray is a people person full of energy and enthusiasm.

Hello, Ray. Let's go way back to your marketing experience beginnings.

Through high school and college I was a disk jockey, and mostly worked in radio and television. I was a clown on TV and I was a rock and roll disc jockey in Tucson at the University of Arizona. I knew quite a bit about radio and TV when I graduated from college.

What was your major?

I majored in Marketing, with an emphasis in Advertising, and when I went to Phoenix I was an account executive. I was done being a disc jockey at that point. I just wanted to go out and sell.

17

Were you a disc jockey while you were going to school?

I sure was. I was in radio and television when I was going to college. I always worked and went to school at the same time and I learned a lot about the media. I was a prop boy at my first job in television. I had to set up displays and all that sort of thing. We didn't even have videotape. Everything was live back in the late 1950's. That was the very beginning of it and it was great. It was the golden age of TV.

You learned the real basics.

It was a time when nobody really knew what they were doing in television. I was there when television started in Tucson in 1953. I started in television about five years after that. It was very crude. For example, I worked for a CBS station and we couldn't run the Ed Sullivan Show since there was no videotape yet. You couldn't tape delay anything, so we'd get it on film a week later. When Elvis appeared on national television we saw him a week later. It was live on the network, but when you were in the west and Elvis appeared at seven o'clock they didn't want him to appear at five o'clock. They wanted him to appear at the right time. I also had a rock and roll record company and produced records in high school. In college I would buy six hours of radio time as a disc jockey and I would go out and sell it to other people and remote broadcasts. After I graduated from college I came to Phoenix and I started selling radio advertising. Then I moved over to selling television; that's when I really found the power of the media. In those days, media and television were very powerful. In every market there were only three or four television stations. Therefore when you advertised on one channel or two channels in town, you got massive results. It was fabulous! In 1972 I quit my job and started my own advertising agency. I would go out and I would work for various clients.

Did you specialize in any type of client?

Primarily retail. I had a partner. As a matter of fact, my partner today is the same partner I had back in the early 1970's.

So, did you primarily use TV with these retailers?

We did. We were really strong with television. Then we got involved in those starving artist types of sales that nobody had ever done before. It all started when an art gallery went out of business in Phoenix. We had the guy come to us and say, "I sold my business. I don't want to be in this anymore. The guy who bought it from me reneged on the payment. Would you do a going out of business sale?" We thought a going out of business sale for an art gallery would be interesting. He said it was art that he had gotten overseas, like inexpensive paintings. They were good paintings. They just came from overseas and they were cheap. It was amazing the markup we could get on that stuff. So we did it. I remember the advertising: "Master's Art Gallery of Scottsdale closes its doors. The entire remaining stock will be sold at 80 percent off the retail price." We had lines around the block for that thing. It was incredible! A light bulb lit up and we thought, "What if we just took this on the road and did it in other markets?" We took a whole load of the paintings and brought them down to Tucson. In our advertisement we said: "Master's Art Gallery of Scottsdale has closed its doors! The total remaining stock has been shipped to the Ramada in Tucson for this one time only sale." People were lined up around the block. It was incredible! No one had ever seen anything like this before. We did one market after another and every place we went we blew the doors down. We did it all over the country and all over the world. We did it in Australia, New Zealand, Canada, England, and even in Venezuela and Mexico. I did the same art sales in Guadalajara, so I had somebody to translate it for me. Instead of the guy saying, "Oil paintings," it translated as, "Grease paintings!" [Laughs.]

(Laughs) You had an American translator!

By the mid 1980's I had done a lot of things on the road besides the oil paintings. Everyone got into the oil painting business and all of a sudden there was somebody else doing the same thing. They would copy my ads word for word in radio and television. I decided to try women's shoes, clothing, gold and leather goods.

Did you have a road show for each of these things?

Yes, books too. I bought this whole book warehouse and it was the worst business ever. Have you ever needed to move books? It was the worst, no kidding! Oh, that was an awful business. Then we got hooked up with a guy whose name was Paul Simon. Not the singer. This Paul Simon was involved in real estate. In the mid 1980's there was a guy who offered a "no money down" real estate deal. He came to us and asked if we could help him with his advertising. We made a big media campaign that said, "Come to the free lecture. Learn how to buy property with no money down and turn it into an instant income with the stroke of a pen." Then at the end of his pitch, he would sell his home study course for about $300. He was pretty good at it. For a while we created a media campaign for him and became his partner on a 50-50 basis. We were fairly successful. We would hire people to be speakers and send them out on the road. We had about four or five road shows. For example I had one African American guy and he would go and promote to the African American communities. We would advertise on Reverend Ike's radio show. We had all the bases covered on this thing. You used to be able to go into a television market in Dallas, Phoenix, Fresno, Bakersfield or Sacramento and buy two of the four TV stations and the coverage would be fantastic! After cable TV came along the ratings weren't quite as good, because all of a sudden people had a lot of channels in their home. I thought with cable TV I could take the whole lecture, put it on television and invite people to come and watch it. At the end of the televised lecture I could sell them the books and tapes. I didn't have to get them to a hotel ballroom anymore! That was the first infomercial.

You were able to test for a lot less money with cable?

Yes. So I thought that if I was going to test this thing in some oddball market, nobody's going to be aware of the fact that we're doing it. In those days, not a lot of markets had really strong cable. Urban areas hadn't really gotten involved with cable yet. I picked Lowell, Massachusetts as my market because there was about 80 percent cable penetration. I bought time on their local cable station and ran this program maybe 12 times. Then I ran a big ad in the Lowell newspaper saying, "Learn how to buy real estate with no money down. Watch at these certain times." After that weekend the response was fabulous! I couldn't believe it. I went out and I borrowed money from everyone I could find. I did a national campaign. Some networks aren't even around anymore like the Satellite Program Network. I also ran it on The Nashville Network and USA. All those cable stations were just starting in those days. The first weekend after I ran my program on the national network, I'd sold a million dollars worth of tapes.

Did you get a merchant account for that?

Yes.

Was that a problem for you at all?

It was no problem. At that time we were affiliated with a bank and we ran them right through the bank. At one time we were The Arizona Bank's largest merchant. Subsequently it's been difficult. It was such a huge success and we kept on buying more time. I had to get more space and hire employees. Then all of a sudden we were doing a lot of shows. I got Tom Hopkins, the real estate guru. I had Zig Ziglar on a TV show and the late Charles Givens. I had about twenty or thirty shows on the air.

Did Zig Ziglar sell his books and tapes?

Yes. I had all these people doing this stuff and it was a huge success. I'm known as the guy who first started the infomercial. In 1986 I got a huge offer from somebody back in Philadelphia who wanted to buy my company and I sold it. It went on the New York Stock Exchange and it was a fabulous deal. Then I got in the 900 number business for a while, which was incredible but only lasted about three years. After that I started doing more retail and bought some radio stations in Nevada, where I also owned some retail stores. I was selling watches and jewelry and all kinds of things in casinos. A few years ago I decided I was going to start working on the Internet.

Are the watches that the casinos sell already made or are they made per order?

They are already made. I have stores in casinos where I sell watches and jewelry. I was doing that when the Internet started gaining popularity. Back in 1996 or 1997 I went out and I got the domain name TheWatchman.com.

You were right in there at the beginning.

It was hard to find somebody who knew how to build a website. I got somebody who said they knew how to build a website and they really didn't. They just wanted to take my money! That's the way it was in those days.

It takes a long time and a lot of money to build a good website.

Well, I built this huge website and nobody went to it, so I took it down. A few years later, I decided to try eBay because a friend of mine had some success with his eBay program. I started selling watches on eBay and we've been doing it in a large way for about two years, although we still have the retail stores.

You get 50 million people visiting the site and that's what you want, circulation.

Did you start out with the same concept that you have now with a variety of faces on the watches? Different graphics?

Yes. I liked the idea of the custom watches with the faces and everything. I also wanted to sell name brand watches like Citizen, Seiko and Bulova. I didn't want the Rolex type, but not Timex either. I had access to really good prices for the middle brands and thought I could sell them and make some money.

But on eBay you're focused on using custom graphics on the faces of your watches.

That is correct. For a while I could make money on watches without custom faces, but because so many other people are selling the same watches I couldn't make money with them. I could get fabulous bargains on the watches. But when you get a lot of people selling the same thing on eBay, it brings the price down. It's not worth paying $50 for a watch and selling it for $60. You need to be to at least double your money on that thing. A businessman has to do that in order to cover his overhead.

Are most of your auctions three days?

They're seven days and they have to be reposted. Some services can't do that for you. We were thinking about switching to Vendio, and they said, "Oh we can't re-post for you." It's mandatory in our business to have a service that can repost everything.

That's the whole intention of having a service. So you have a starting price that is considerably lower than the Buy-It-Now price. Is that right?

That's correct.

Do you have a reserve in there as well?

No.

Are you just letting it float the way it wants to go?

That's correct. We've experimented a lot in the past with that.

Are there any other options that eBay offers which you use?

We use the gallery photo and we're considering not even using the gallery photo anymore.

Your descriptions paint a pretty good picture of your items.

Yes. The customers need to see the watch. If you type in the words "Lizzie Borden" all the Lizzie Borden stuff comes up. Then our watch would be seen. It costs a lot to run that little picture on the side there. I'm not talking about the main picture in the listing, I'm talking about the little gallery photo. They cost up to 30 cents. When you're running 4,000 listings a week that's a lot of money. We're considering dropping that option.

On your website watchesbythedozen.com you have custom watches.

We make watches for people and we do special orders.

That's a nice concept. It's a matter of driving traffic in there. Right?

Well, with eBay you can drive traffic to another site. You have to be careful how you do it because they have certain rules. For example, in your listing page you can't take somebody from your watch listing to your website, but you can take them to your "About Me" page. From there, you can take them to another site. eBay is very restrictive. But all in all, eBay is sensational.

I haven't seen TheWatchman.com. Is that website still running?

Yes. That's really just an informational site about the retail stores. It has a web cam and it shows our store, but we don't sell anything on that site. This site shows a quote from Bill Geist, a correspondent for the *CBS Evening News*. He said "The Watch Man sells more watches than anybody—anywhere!"

Do you sell much overseas?

Absolutely. About twenty percent of our business is overseas in mostly English speaking nations. I've actually sold to most countries in the world. We've been to all the interesting Baltic states. If you have a picture of the president of Kazakstan on the watch, perhaps they'd like to buy it in Kazakstan.

Do you sell custom watches on eBay?

No. We don't sell custom watches on eBay.

When you originally started your website years ago, there were no search engines and therefore no pay-per-click or banner advertising. Right?

Right. There was no Google and no Yahoo. They are really big and doing very well now. I think eBay is king of them all. I know a lot of people have been very successful with eBay, because they have created a fabulous shopping mall. You get fifty million people visiting the site and that's what you want, circulation.

Where do you see the Internet going?

I see a combination of television and the Internet. We're probably going to see streaming video, because there are so many live things right now on the Internet. You have to have high speed Internet to really see them. Pretty soon we're going to have millions of channels.

Do you think we'll have a combination of computer and TV and Internet access all in one?

That's right. It's virtually here right now. I have a personal website, I have a website for my high school class, and I have a website for another group in Phoenix. I don't think there's really a need to have libraries anymore, because the information you want can be found on the Internet.

Do you see anything eBay might be adding to their program in the near future?

I see them tweaking their site all the time; making things easier, better, more convenient. Whatever they do, they're doing it right. The fact of the matter is that there are some people who are making money on eBay. I bet you the majority of people are having fun and getting rid of stuff or they're doing it as a hobby. Making money is a difficult thing to do unless you're really clever. If you're just a regular guy and every Saturday you go around to garage sales and look for stuff you want to put up on eBay, you won't make very much money. It's pretty work intensive but you have a lot of fun with it and maybe make a couple of dollars. I bet most of eBay users are like that.

When you first started did you have somebody else load eBay for you?

No. A friend of mine told me about it and I thought I would give it a try. I had a Kenneth Cole watch and was reading the directions on eBay. eBay said I needed someone to host my picture. It was pretty complicated. So I stuck the watch in my scanner and scanned a picture of it!

Did it come out okay?

Well, it wasn't too bad. I put it in there and I got the pricing all screwed up. Where it said "price" I thought they meant the retail price, not what I wanted to start it with. I put the retail price of the watch, which was $135, and then after a week I couldn't figure out why I didn't get any bids on it. (Laughs) I was kind of embarrassed so I just set it aside for about 6 months. Then I learned how to do it and eBay got easier. They got to be a lot more consumer-friendly. Their explanations became easier. They share the basics of HTML and explain that if you use little symbols you can create paragraphs and if you use other little symbols you can create other affects. It's really easy. I tried it for a while, and by gosh, I sold everything and I made money from it all. I was really happy. We custom made quite a few watches. I had one that said "Crazy about Croquet." It showed a guy playing croquet. I put it on eBay and it sold for $100 (Laughs).

[Laughs.] Since there are 50 million people looking at eBay somebody's going to buy it!

Especially if they play croquet and never saw this watch before. They didn't know if I was ever going to put it up again. I put it up the next week, and the next week it sold for seventy-five! The next week it sold for fifty, the next week it sold for thirty and about twelve weeks later I ran out of the product. I feel sorry for the guy who bought it first for $100, but he didn't know if it would ever be up there again.

Where did you start the bid?

A dollar.

And they bid it right on up to a hundred.

Yes. As a matter of fact in those days, I was starting every bid at a dollar!

Did you have any reserve then?

No. No reserve.

So you just let it go the way it's going to go.

I just let it go, you bet.

If somebody wants to get into eBay as a business can you think of attributes or mental attitudes they ought to have?

Well, I think the key thing is the product. You've got to have the right product. Do you want to get into eBay to make money, to try and really make it a good moneymaking venture? I suppose everybody has that in mind, but I'm sure there are a lot of people that do it for fun. I have another site that I use just for my own personal items. I put a few items on there, things that I buy and sell. It's totally separate. I have a few watches up and I start everything at a dollar. It's so much fun to watch your things go up everyday. I have Phoenix Suns basketball tickets that I sell during the basketball season. Reneé, my fiancée will say, "Oh! Go in there and bid on this thing!" I'll go in there and it's just a lot of fun. But getting back to the question you asked, I said the product is the most important thing. You've got to find a product that you can have a ready supply of all the time. If you're going to sell single products or inexpensive one-of-a-kind products, it's really time consuming. You have to take a picture of it. Then you have to write a description. Then you have to post it on eBay and then you have to send it out. Once you've sold a "one of a kind" item the picture's no good anymore, the description's no good anymore, and for the next item you've got to write it up all over again. So you need to get quite a few of the same thing. There's a certain economy of scale. If you look at my ZoomDeluxe.com, you'll see several watches that I have. They're all Citizen brand. I have about two-dozen of each one of those watches. After one sells, I put up another one. All I do is just click and it's up there again.

Are you familiar with a Dutch auction? How does that work?

Yes. I know what you're talking about. It's a little hazy and I've tried it on occasion. If you have twelve of one item you can put them all up at once, but I find with more expensive items I like to do them one at a time.

Do you have the same items in your store as you do listed?

Not necessarily. For example, on eBay I can have a picture of the Communist Russia flag with the hammer and sickle. And it'll sell; it's a great seller. Maybe people long for communism, I don't know. But if I took the same item and I put it in my store

27

it would probably offend people. Nobody would ever buy it. (Laughs). So you have to be careful with that stuff. I'll tell you an interesting story though. I can put all kinds of things at my retail stores and nobody will ever buy them because I'll never reach the right person. When I put something on eBay, it will find its own market. A person who collects items having to do with the old west, let's take Doc Holliday, a guy who collects Doc Holliday stuff is always putting the words "Doc Holliday" in search engines to see what comes up. When he does, he'll find my watch. But I could have that watch in my store for ten years and never sell it. I had a Seiko watch and it was an ugly watch I had paid about $100 for. I started out trying to get $300 in my store. Then I had it marked down to $200, then $150. Finally I had it marked down to $100. I just wanted to get out of it, because it was such an ugly watch. So I put it on eBay and it sold for $500, because it was an odd collector's watch from Japan. Nobody here was interested in it, but for some reason they collected that watch in Japan. A lot of people will wander around swap meets and look for unusual things. But I say again, in order to have something that's really unusual and to be able to post it over and over again, you have to be really clever about how you do it.

Is there anything else that you would like to add?

Well, it's just a fabulous way for people to do marketing. It's like being offered a space in a shopping mall. eBay just wants a little bit when you sell, so just give them a little bit to put your item in there and you're in business. You don't have to spend $500,000 building a store! It's wonderful. Everybody's protected with the great feedback system and always very careful. You want to make sure that you're a hundred percent and that people like you. I've not been troubled with any fraud at all. It's just worked out. It's the greatest. I have such a great belief in it.

When I put something on eBay, it will find its own market.

How many people do you have to manage this for you?

At one time I had about twelve people working for me. I have about half of that right now. That's because I took out a whole layer of expensive watches. We just do the inexpensive watches now. You have to ship all this stuff out. The people who have really made a lot of money from this whole deal are the shipping people! This has been a bonanza for Federal Express and UPS and the United States Postal Service.

How do you find people?

In the small town we're in we have regular employees for the stores. We run ads in the paper and you'd be surprised how many people will call. When we first started I wanted photographers. All that their job required was to take pictures. It's hard to take pictures of watches. They're such little things and they don't come out very well. People looking for work are always interested in this type of thing.

You have a lot of knowledge and experience. Have you ever thought of sharing it?

I used to go out and give a speech on how to start a business. I often think about writing a book on it because I have a lot of interesting credentials. I have quotes from various magazines and television shows and stuff like that. The thing is I know how to start businesses for almost nothing.

Karen McMasters

Goal Setting Gives Her a Target

She feels if she can do it, anyone can. Karen McMasters had no sales, marketing or Internet experience before starting her business. She didn't even have a computer at home. By setting goals, Karen has been able to stay on course. She has created a lifestyle others just dream of.

You mentioned that you started out by selling some of your used baby items and clothing on eBay? Were these just items that you had no more use for?

Yes. My daughter had grown up.

Had you done anything on eBay up to that point?

No.

So this was totally new to you.

Yes. I just heard about it and thought I'd try it, and it worked well.

31

It worked well, and then you started selling items for neighbors and so on?

Yes. Then I started going to garage sales and picking up more items.

That's probably the hard part.

Yes. That was the hard part. It took a lot of the time. Half of the time I would get home and something would be wrong with the items.

Part of a learning curve, I guess!

Yes. That's why I opened the online store BareBabies.com. I got tired of cleaning up items and finding broken things I hadn't noticed before. I decided to just sell new things.

Still, it's amazing how many things you can find at garage sales.

Yeah, it is amazing.

But it's a lot of hard work. Did you have Internet experience prior to doing this?

No. We just started the business. I didn't have a computer at home, so I got one.

Well, you were really quite a novice then.

Yes. I was good on the computers at work, but I wasn't on the Internet. I understood email and the software programs for accounting purposes or sales. So as far as the Internet goes, I wasn't familiar–a little bit of online shopping, but not nearly what I know now.

You worked for an artist named Wyland, correct?

Yes. He's an environmental sea life artist. He paints murals and he has art galleries all over the world. He has quite a few of them in Hawaii, a couple of them in the San Diego area (one in Seaport Village and one in La Jolla), a couple in Laguna Beach and many of them in Florida. He has a goal to do 100 "Whaling Wall" sea life murals in the United States by the year 2010. I think he's on number 80 or 90 now. When he completes 100, he's done. That was his goal. It's taking him many, many years to do that.

Were you doing office work there? Were you doing any marketing?

No marketing and no sales. All office work.

And before that?

Well, was there life before that? [Laughs.] I worked for an aerospace company.

Interesting. So you really had no marketing or Internet background?

No. I didn't leave my position thinking I was going to go start my own business either. I never even had that thought in my mind at all. It just happened. I quit working in Wyland's office five years ago, but I consulted for him for a year. All of this eBay selling started about five years ago. I goofed around for a year on eBay - just goofing around side money. Then in February of 2000, I opened my online baby store, BareBabies.com. I actually had an online store on EarthLink, and then I switched over to Yahoo after about a year.

Did you design the EarthLink website yourself?

I designed it myself.

So then you thought, "Hey, this is some great software, I can create a neat site!"

Yes! Yahoo has some really great templates.

I've looked at those templates, and it looks like they give end users a lot of flexibility.

Yeah they do. I've found a place that does design work for Yahoo stores, which makes life much easier and it makes it look really professional. They're called Solid Cactus. So now I can keep up with the big guys instead of looking like a little Yahoo store.

I've checked out your website and I really like the maneuverability. It was very easy to navigate. Where do you find the pictures?

I get disks from the manufacturers. A reputable manufacturer will have a disk for you featuring pictures of their products. So all the pictures are professional and clear. We don't have our own photographer or anything.

They look very professional.

Thank you. I do modify them quite a bit. I may shrink them, or if there are different colors, I'll make little swatches and put them on the inset photos. I also edit pictures I've taken and cut up with PhotoShop, and just put those together. For instance, you'll have one picture showing the product and four color options for that product. If that's the case, you show an inset picture with four swatches of the different colors. I've learned a lot about modifying pictures with PhotoShop.

Have you had to modify any other aspects of your websites?

Yes. I'm changing Ciao Bella Baby right now. People who visit that site are having trouble navigating, because on the left-hand side of the page you see a big stroller and the big highchair and people don't know where to go. They think we've only got strollers and highchairs. They don't know that when you click on the picture, we have quite a few other items there. They don't think we have very many products in that store when we have the same amount as we do in BareBabies, which is close to 900. Soon there will be a whole new navigation bar on the left-hand side of Ciao Bella Baby with words, similar to how it is at Bare Babies.

Are there identical products lines for both sites?

You know...we don't move the products that don't sell well over to Ciao Bella Baby. Only our best sellers are at Ciao Bella Baby.

And the pricing is the same?

It has to be, yes. Because the manufacturer controls the pricing.

What does Yahoo give you for the monthly fee they charge?

The server. Your store is on their server. It's a good value because they're big and they know what they're doing. So if anything happens in the Internet world, like viruses or attacks, they can recover your system quickly. We don't have to pay for a server, which can be very expensive! You also are provided with advertising–they do quite a bit for you with advertising. They have Yahoo Shopping, which we chose to be in, and great customer support. The customer support is the biggest thing. It's only $299.95 a month and there's a certain percentage you pay for each sale.

So of the three programs that Yahoo has, you've got the top program, but you pay less per sale?

Percentage-wise, yes. For bigger stores it's a better deal to use the Merchant Professional option.

You just calculate out your volumes of sales to see what's most ideal?

Yes.

Basically, you get the same service with each of these programs?

Yes. In my Cola store, we have selected the lowest program, because that's more affordable for that particular store. And yes, we get the same service, the same customer support people, and the same offers. I get all the same offers. Every time a new offer comes up, it's for all three stores.

The only products I'm selling on eBay are things I can't resell as new.

Did you start out with a smaller store first and then graduate up to a bigger one?

Yes. Yahoo just came out with their tiered program about a year ago. I didn't have a smaller store before. It was all $49.95 a month before and then there were fees for Yahoo Store orders with separate fees for all orders. So, any order that you got from a Yahoo network they would charge you for. Plus, they would charge you a fee for any other order that you received from anywhere else. Now they've changed to this three-tiered program, where you can choose whatever price you want and then you only have to pay the transaction fee. You don't pay separately for Yahoo Store orders.

Well, technical support is always worth a lot, particularly when you can actually talk to somebody. Do you also get your own merchant account?

Yes. They offer you one called Paymentech. You sign up through Yahoo when you start a store. You can go with others, but you have to make sure they're affiliated with Yahoo. Yahoo does have an affiliate program, as well. While you're signing up for their store, you can sign up for the affiliate program, and they approve it.

So it features the best online security that's available? I know people don't prefer to use their credit cards unless they're assured they will be protected. That's important.

Yes. It does provide great security. It is important.

So that gives you some reliable backing. With your advertising, you're primarily doing a pay-per-click?

Yes.

So you don't pay anything unless somebody goes to your website?

Correct.

Are these statistics primarily tabulated on Google and Yahoo?

It's done through Overture. Google is affiliated with AOL and Overture is affiliated with Yahoo. Yahoo owns Overture now. Yahoo is its own entity, but your account is handled through Overture.

Is it similar to a banner ad?

No. If you go to Yahoo.com and type anything in the search box, when you click "search," it brings up sponsored listings as text not banners.

So it's basically like a search engine ...

Yes, but you have control over where you're showing up. You always want to show up in the top three or four search results, so you're sure to show up on the first page.

Of course, they want you to get clicks.

Yes. That's how they make their money.

So you don't pay anything unless you get clicks. That works well. Do you happen to know what percentage of people who visit your site actually purchase from you?

You know, it's really hard for us to gauge. We do have conversion rate statistics set up for those sites. Still, it's hard to gauge. Especially in the baby industry. People find out they're pregnant and they visit us, but they're looking. However, they still have nine or ten months' time until they need to make a purchase. So they'll come in and maybe do a baby registry on our site or it's Grandma looking for her grandbaby. Conversion is really hard in this business, because it's not an impulse buy we're talking about. It's a thought-out purchase, and our customers really shop before they buy. Think about it: just because that person clicked in January, they might not actually purchase the product until August or September. By that point, we can't track statistics. Also, they could have forwarded an email or a link to Grandma to buy the stroller. Tracking and statistics get lost in the shuffle. Customers just add us to their registry, and then their friends come into the registry and they buy items online. The conversion rate is really hard to track in our business.

Do you sell many gift certificates?

No. That's weird, isn't it?

That surprises me.

We put information about gift certificates on the front page, because we want to sell them. I mean, it's a great deal. We say, "Look! We have this on our front page! Gift certificates. Send them to the receiver. Come on…." Still, everyone is just shopping for specific items. I think people want to physically buy something, especially a baby shower gift.

Your gift certificates range from $20 to $1,000. That pretty much catches the whole gamut for almost anybody.

Yeah. We've never sold a $1,000 gift certificate. I think the biggest gift certificate we've ever sold is $500.

Well, if you add it up, $1,000 really isn't that much.

Oh, yeah. It's a good stroller, a car seat and a highchair. That's about it.

Let's say a customer buys a stroller. Do you have a customer database that says, "Jane bought a stroller on such and such a day," or information that can be used for mailers?

We do, but we don't do it unless customers opt into our mailing list. It's basically illegal to contact anyone via email or U.S. mail who hasn't really asked for it. We do have options to sign up for our mailing list on both of our sites. At the top and the bottom of our home page, there are links that read, "mailing list." If you click on them, it'll take you to a page where you can sign up. There are also links on the bottom that say "bookmark this page" or "send this page to a friend," so people can forward information about us to others. We also create email newsletters for those people, because it's free. Unless they've signed up on that mailing list, we don't contact them. Spam is illegal, which is amazing considering how many spam emails you get in a day, and it's spamming if you do it without consent. Businesses will sell email addresses to people too! And you think, "Okay, how did this person get my email address?" Businesses sell their lists. We never, ever sell our lists. We had somebody call the other day wanting to switch lists or buy our lists. I said, "Sorry.

We don't do that." I don't like it. I'm not going to do it to somebody else. We should just get everyone in the world thinking that way.

Can a person join your mailing list without being a customer?

Yes.

Just by signing up?

Yes, and that's another thing. Visitors want to know if we have sales coming up, but when they're first signing up, they're just looking…seeing what's out there and what they're going to want in nine months.

So that's automatically an opt-in?

Yes. That's an opt-in, and that's not illegal, because they ask for it. In the "checkout" part of the process, it says, "Would you like to get our newsletter?" They can opt-in that way.

Are most people opting in to get their newsletter?

No. More people come in via the mailing lists, then they click "check out" and subscribe to the newsletter. Just because they placed an order doesn't mean they want the newsletter. In fact, half of our customers write on their orders, "Do not send me anything. Do not sell my information." People are paranoid. They don't want anything but their order confirmation and their tracking number. I don't blame them. I don't want anything else either. If I shop somewhere, just send me my order and my confirmation number. If I want something, I'll come back.

Yes. They are aware. They've looked through your site, and they can go back in again. Unless you have some unbelievably revolutionary product, there's no real reason to email them, because they already know where to go.

Well, my philosophy is, "I don't like spam, I'm not going to spam somebody else." You know, I've had buyers come in and say, "Oh! We should use your list; it's 20,000 people! We should use it or at least send out an opt-in letter." We tried it once and hardly anyone opted in. Everyone is so sick of spam. Nobody wants to opt into anything because they're afraid that one opt-in causes a thousand emails.

Are most of your manufacturers drop shipping?

They drop ship about 60 percent of our products.

And the other 40 percent you store in a warehouse?

Yes.

Do you try to stock everything?

No. We don't stock our biggest seller, which is Peg Perego. There have been others that we decided to stock because the manufacturer was having a really hard time drop shipping, and we were having a hard time getting tracking numbers. So we decided just to warehouse the items, because then it's in our hands. In this way, we can get the order out and we have more control over everything. But our biggest manufacturer, Peg Perego, does drop ship for us, and they do a really great job. When the product's on its way we get the tracking number.

So do you stock each of the items that you ship from your warehouse, or do you order them as needed?

We stock each one.

So you have to determine how much of an item to stock depending on the demand for it?

Correct.

Well, that makes things kind of smooth for you then.

Yes.

There's a tracking number when you have something drop shipped. The customer is notified, and you know an item has been sent.

Yes.

Okay. And you're basically collecting the money and paying the manufacturer?

Correct.

So then you open up a credit line?

Yes.

Where do you think the future of Internet marketing is heading?

Our children are learning how to surf the Internet and learning all about computers in school. All those kids are going to grow up, and they won't be afraid of the Internet because they were brought up on it. So I only see it growing immensely. Because right now, you still have people trying out the Internet and they still want to call in their orders. My eight-year-old daughter turns the computer on, logs on to the Internet, and clicks all around. She's eight and she's been doing that for a couple years. Children are not afraid of it. They don't see it as a threat.

Yes. It's like being brought up with TV. We don't think anything of it.

Right! And the computer is just a part of life. It's just something these children we mentioned will have in their homes. Computers. It's exactly what you said about televisions, just something we have in our homes now.

As for the age group for the product lines on your websites, when you say "babies" what age does that include?

We go to about seven years old. Beyond seven years old we're looking at different types of products. Clothing, for example. Especially with girls. Girls are beginning to get into makeup and clothing; for boys it's big bikes. Children get older and their products and needs change. They don't need our products anymore.

Did you have a mentor when you started at all?

No.

You just said, "I'm going to do this. I've got these used baby items and…"

And I'm just going to do it! Just goofing around.

And you're still using eBay for returns that you need to sell?

Yes.

Do you have a minimum bid or reserve price? How are you structuring that, generally?

I do both, especially if it's a costly product. Like, for a high-end double stroller or something similar, I always put a reserve on it. I make sure the price is at least the same as what I paid for it, because I don't want to lose money on it. The only products I'm selling on eBay are things I can't resell as new. Here's an example. We got back a stroller the other day. The chassis was scratched up. So I sold it on eBay and I wrote, "The chassis is scratched up." It was a return to our warehouse. It wasn't used, but the chassis was scratched during the shipment. I specified that, and they know they're getting a deal. Those usually go really fast. I do usually put a reserve on something that's high dollar. I don't want to lose money.

Could you just start the bid at that price and not have a reserve?

You're going to have more bidders when you start at a lower price because people think, "Oh, cool! Look. This is $9.99." They know there's a reserve on the item. But then they bid, just for bidding's sake. And then they'll have somebody bid against them. And they'll say, "No, this is mine!" And then they bid again. So that process gets the bidding going because if you flat out say, "This item costs four hundred dollars," they say, "Ugh," and don't bid on anything. Otherwise this bidding war begins, and then customers get competitive. Sometimes you can create both a reserve price and a Buy-It-Now price. After the customer meets the reserve, the Buy-It-Now goes away. People do this bidding and they could have bought the item for less if they had just paid the Buy-It-Now price before it was removed. Sometimes, you'll end up making more money than if you'd sold it at the Buy-It-Now price.

So, you're generally not using the Buy-It-Now feature?

I do use Buy-It-Now. Absolutely.

All three. So you start with a low opening minimum bid and include a reserve price and a Buy-It-Now price. If the reserve is met then the Buy-It-Now is removed and the bidding may actually go higher. Is that right?

Yes! The Buy-It-Now goes away when the reserve is met. The bidders don't even know there was a Buy-It-Now option, and they're just bidding. They're just going at it and fighting against each other until 20 seconds before the auction is over! I've seen times when customers paid more than what the full retail price would be in my store, because they got into a bidding war. Not often, but it has happened. And I feel bad about it. I think, "Oh, my gosh! They could have gotten it brand new in the store for twenty dollars cheaper!" I feel totally bad, because they just got into this heated bidding war and just lost their mind.

It shows you have some good items that people want.

Yes. And that's what I did when I went to garage sales. I started saying, "Oh! That Peg Perego's popular! And, that's a good resale value." You know what I mean? There were some strollers by certain manufacturers that I learned to stay away from, because they were lower-end or lower quality strollers. Nobody pays peanuts for those resale. Sometimes I lost. I'd say, "Oh! I'll pay twenty dollars for something at a garage sale and I couldn't sell it on eBay for twenty dollars." So I learned from reselling the baby products that were high-end and popular. Now I know what brands to go after. The first brand I went after was Peg Perego. I flew to Dallas to get the account. I knew that was a good resale item on eBay, so it must be a really good product. And it was selling for a lot of money. I picked up a Peg Perego highchair once at a garage sale for twenty-five dollars. I sold it on eBay for a hundred and twenty five dollars and it was used! And they sell new online for one fifty nine. I said to myself, "Oh! This Peg Perego stuff is good stuff."

You must've gained a lot of experience in packaging and shipping. Those aren't the easiest things to ship.

I was hunting for boxes in trashcans. There was no way I was going to pay retail for a box! That would cut into my profit margins. My husband and I would take his truck and we came to know the good trashcans!

What does he think of your business? Is he pretty supportive?

Yes. Absolutely.

And is he Internet savvy at all?

Not at all. He tries, but, you know, he'll say, "I couldn't get in the other day." I said, "You must have typed something wrong." And then it's, "No. I know how to spell racquetball!" (Laughs) I got home and I said, "You forgot the 'c' before the 'q.'" And he says, "Ah! Why didn't I see that?" I mean, it's so easy to mis-type something, you know, in the URL. So, he tries, but it's...a little too frustrating for him. He's never been that way. He's into sports and he's a bail bond agent. So he's in a whole different world than I am.

Do you see yourself doing any international sales or do you do any?

Never. No way. It's just too hard to ship. You know, you've got to do all the customs paperwork. Especially now. It's a nightmare. We did a little bit in the beginning. People begged us. I think I worked with a girl in Australia a couple of times, but it's just too much of a hassle. We don't do international shipping.

When you set up your original site did you get software to help you?

Yes. I used a template.

Did you have any kind of a budget when you started?

I didn't plan. I didn't get a loan. I just started with credit cards.

Okay. So you said, "Hey, I'm going for it." Costs came up, and you said, "Okay, now I've got to do this, and I've got to do that."

[Laughs.] Yes. I have no business sense whatsoever. Still have no business sense!

What kind of person do you think would be most successful in starting their own online business like you have?

Somebody that's motivated. A go-getter. I don't ever stop. I go. I go. I go. I mentioned earlier that I didn't have any business experience. No marketing or sales experience. I don't think experience is what you need. I just think you need to be semi-intelligent and a hard worker. That's something I can definitely claim to be.

Do you get many returns?

Yes, because we sell a lot. We probably get, I don't know, one or two a day. Sometimes they're used items, too.

What do you do then? Just say, "Okay, we'll resell those used items," and take them back?

It depends. Our website states an item "…has to be brand new," and sometimes we'll have stuff come back with animal hair on it. An item has to be returned in good condition. That's pretty much industry standard for retail stores.

Are you ever overstocked in any particular item?

Sometimes we'll drop a product line. We're dropping a line right now because they've decided to go into Target. So I've refused to carry their product anymore. I've discounted all their products and they're going out the door. There are situations like that. I don't do a lot of sales. But if you see a sale, it's because something's happening. Like the product line I mentioned, for instance. Since they're transitioning to Target, we're phasing them out.

What about advertising your website in newspapers? Have you tried any print ads?

Yes. We've probably been in three different magazines. One did okay. That's another thing. It's hard to tell where people actually saw us. We did do print ads in *Pregnancy* magazine, for instance. Print ads don't work nearly as well as the Internet, because customers are already on the Internet and they're looking. For them to take that magazine over to the computer is something else entirely. Or they may see an ad in the doctor's office and don't remember it by the time they get home.

Are there some other areas on the Internet that you pursued other than pay-per-click?

Comparison shopping. Shopping.com, Epinions.com and PriceGrabber.com. Those do pretty well for us, too.

Are there some things that didn't work for you?

Pretty much everything's worked on the Internet. Basically you get what you pay for. I may think, "So, I paid the hundred bucks and didn't see anything from it." Then I don't do it again. The things we're doing are working, so we just continue to do it.

I've seen times when customers paid more than what the full retail price would be in my store.

Well, with the pay-per-click at least you know you're only paying if people visit you. With banner ads, you really don't know, do you?

Right. We did do some banner advertising and didn't get a lot of action. I think most people stay away from banners. I know I do. I don't click on banners because you never know what's going to pop up anymore.

Right. Not to bring back any bad memories, but what do you think is the worst day that you've had? Is there any day that stands out, where you thought, "Hey, this was not a good day. This isn't what I wanted ..."

No. Well, we've had customers every once in a while that can be challenging, but I'm sure that happens in any business. We'll turn around and we'll have another customer that says, "You guys have the best website, and your navigation's great," and we say, "Somebody loves us."

Any day that stands out as being an exceptional day?

The *USA Today* article. That was very exciting for me.

To be featured in an article...*USA Today* and also *Entrepreneur* magazine, that's great!

Yeah. The *Entrepreneur* magazine article took months before it went to print. So I think I had a long time to be excited about it and then absorb it. And then it came out and we said, "Oh cool! It's out." But the *USA Today* article happened really fast. They did that interview on Wednesday, and the photo was taken on Friday. Then it came out on a Monday. So it was just very fast. Afterwards we said, "Oh, my gosh! It happened!"

It must have been quite a thrill.

It was a shock! I ran back in and bought the rest of the papers. I was waiting for the cashier to ask, "Why are you buying these?" I kept looking at him, thinking, "Come on! Ask me, ask me." I can't believe I didn't tell him. I left with my big stack of papers. And then I went around to every single 7-Eleven and every single *USA Today* stand in the area, and I picked up about 40 of them.

Where do you think your business is going to be in five or ten years?

Probably more than double, I would think. People are always going to have babies. So I only see the business growing. I feel like our name, Bare Babies, is becoming more branded as each year goes on. I mean, I run into people now and they'll say, "Oh, you own a baby store?" And I say, "Yes," and mention the name. "Oh, I've seen that!" they'll say! I'll answer, "You have? Cool!" So it's amazing how we've become more known and branded because we're still there. I've been there four years now. Customers can even be on their second or third baby and they type Peg Perego in a search engine, and there's BareBabies again. They've heard of us before. So as far as we're concerned, our business is growing and growing every year. Every year we've grown by half a million dollars. That's success. So I only see everyone doing the same, because people are getting more comfortable.

Do you think you'll do over two million dollars this year?

I'm shooting for that. Oh, no, two and a half million. We did two last year.

All right! Well, I can't see it doing anything but, just like you said, getting better. When I was looking through your site and comparing it to walking into a department store and looking at a clutter of baby items, it was so much easier to shop on your website. A lot of it just has to do with the way you've designed that. And again, the quality of the photographs.

You have to have that quality because, if you don't, you're going to get a zillion returns. And they'll say, "I thought it was brown!" That's because computer screen colors are different. So, even that can be a little sticky sometimes. I know that some of our returns exist because customers weren't able to see what the colors look like. What I hope a lot of the shoppers do is go into a store and see a product. Then I hope they end up coming back and shopping online with us, because they don't have to pay tax unless they're in California. For instance, they go look at an item in New York and they don't want to lug it home in a taxi. They're pregnant, so they shop with us. That way items are delivered to their door, with no shipping and no tax. Most of our business is in New York.

Really?

Yes. The East coast. New York and New Jersey. That's where the majority of our high-end sales come from.

Why do you think that is?

Money. Prestige. The products we sell…it's what they all want to be seen using in Central Park.

Interesting. If someone is thinking about starting their own Internet business, are there any suggestions you can think of mentioning to them?

I'd just say, just go for it! Try it.

Great. To the point.

Everybody that I've worked with on the Internet has found success. I'd just tell them to follow the path. I've often thought of writing a book called Opening a Yahoo Store for Dummies. It's so easy. I even mentioned that in one article, yes, I think it was *USA Today*. I'm an intelligent person...but still, it's so easy. You don't have to know business or to be from business backgrounds or marketing backgrounds. I'm sure if you have all that you're going to do even better.

That's a great answer. Like you said, just go for it.

It's a lot of work, but it's not hard. Does that make sense? I would definitely say, "Do it!"

Johnny Morgan

A Second Career

Pride of Workmanship. It may be that because Johnny Morgan was an Airborne Ranger in the U.S. Army that he knows things have to be right the first time. His fondness of art led him to designing custom signs, when he retired from the Army after 32 years of service. This has led to a flourishing business.

Johnny, I looked through your products on eBay. Do you stock all of the signs that you sell?

No.

Are the signs custom made?

I sit down every morning as we get orders for the signs and figure out which signs we were paid for, make a list, and create them. We usually get them in the mail before the end of the day.

Oh, boy! So you don't exactly know what your production's going to be every day?

No.

How do you make the signs? Do you screen them?

They're computer-generated. We develop the artwork through the computer and a plotter cuts the vinyl, then we cut and weave the vinyl. Once we put together the sign we put it in a box and send it to the post office.

Do you sell strictly on the Internet or do you have walk in sales?

We'll sell to anybody who wants to buy. In addition to eBay we have some items for sale on Amazon. Periodically we put signs up for sale at Yahoo. We operate a website and have a local business as well, which is operated from a shop behind my house. So if somebody calls and wants something, I'll go to them.

I noticed that you had an option for customers to sketch out what they want on the sign, which you customize for them.

Yes. But within limits. If somebody knows what they want and gives us a crude sketch we'll try to put it together for them.

Do you send them a proof or just send the sign and hope it's something the customer will like?

I do send proofs, but I charge for them. I charge $50 an hour to develop artwork, but I can also email a JPEG to a customer.

Is that a small percentage of your sales?

Yes. Very small.

You have so many signs!

You would be amazed by what we sell. I'm amazed everyday by what we sell.

Were you in this business before the Internet?

No. Before I went into this business, I was an Airborne Ranger in the Army.

I'll be darned! So you jumped out of the planes and all that?

For thirty-two years.

Boy, that's great. Are you still fit?

Well, not right now… no. [Laughs.] During one of my last assignments, I worked for the headquarters of the desk log in the basement of the Pentagon. During Desert Storm we prepared briefings everyday for Generals, including General Powell when he was Chairman of the Joint Chiefs of Staff. I had an aptitude for creating artwork and developing briefing charts. I retired shortly after Desert Storm, came home and decided I'd start Texsign, where I could do artwork. I went out and scraped up materials and equipment and started to do some sign work. Now we do vinyl graphics and sell signs and banners. If somebody calls I will develop their artwork for a storefront door or something similar.

Initially you were on the Internet?

Oh, no. This probably predates the Internet by three or four years.

You've been on eBay for around five or six years now?

Yes. It was an opportunity to meet people and develop our sales, although eBay is not a profitable operation. I could not survive from what we do on eBay, because it's terribly expensive. eBay isn't something I would do, if all that I got out of it were profits. You're not going to make a living doing that. You might make a little bit of money, but you're not going to make enough money to support yourself. eBay, however, points our customers to other things.

It brings people into your site?

Yes. Things happen that you would never dream about. For example I have a "Podiatrist Parking Only" sign which reads, "All of them should be shoe'd!" or something to that effect. I got a call one day from the Kentucky Podiatry Association, and a guy said, "We're having a convention. Would you sell us 100 signs?" So I said, "Sure," and I sold him 100 signs. The day after that it was a "Pirates Shopping" sign from Key West, Florida. You never know what will sell and what won't sell.

I was impressed with the quality of the signs described on your website; "Indoor-outdoor, they last a long time."

We need to sell a long-life sign. One of our customers is a local community college. They need the "Handicapped Parking," "Faculty Only," and speed limit signs. The signs that I sell are made from the same material as some of my eBay signs. Some of those signs might be good for ten years, if they don't get vandalized. They are very high quality signs; not substandard, cheap or plastic. I could make a plastic sign for less money that would save me from spending a lot on raw materials, but I would rather go with the qualities I can give. That's always been my philosophy.

You certainly stand behind your product. Do you use any kind of search engine or "pay-per-click" service?

I have experimented with that, but it's never been particularly profitable. In fact, I've never made it work. My son, Rick, is in the business with me and we both have Master Degrees in Business Administration. Believe it or not my undergraduate degree is in Petroleum Engineering. The Army sent me to school a couple of times. My concentration in business school was in Marketing and Rick's was in Information Systems.

What a great combination for the Internet!

Yes, and he's a computer whiz! He built our website and does most of the computer work with eBay, Yahoo and Amazon. I'll do anything that needs to be done, like emptying the trash and sweeping the place. I was surfing the Internet one day, before the Internet was widely available, and discovered eBay. I decided that it could be a great venue for selling signs. However, there are so many people doing it that you can't make any money on eBay unless you sell a lot of items and keep your prices down. That is what eBay is primarily good for.

Do you use anything like a customer database? Do you ever send out promotional emails?

Yes. We have an Access database.

But you don't send emails out to past clients.

No. We don't do that for a couple of reasons. It is prohibited by eBay's Terms of Use, and I don't like to get junk mail. So I won't give it to people.

You don't use AuctionWorks or any type of auction management program?

No. AuctionWorks only hosts our website. We have built our own database to track all of our customer information. AuctionWorks is kind of expensive.

How much does AuctionWorks charge?

They charge per transaction.

It doesn't matter what you have for sale, somebody will buy it if you can get enough people to look at it.

Why did you choose AuctionWorks to host your site?

My son chose it. AuctionWorks is also hosting some of our images so that eBay can have access to them. One of the reasons we're using AuctionWorks is that we need to have somebody whose server is up all the time. We can't have servers that go down during inopportune times and we can't afford to have our system crash and take our images down. We have to be available 24 hours a day, 7 days a week. There's no excuse for downtime. We can't stand that because we have to be up all the time. AuctionWorks has got a good record.

Where do you see this going from here and how do you get the traffic to your site? Is it from repeat sales?

A lot of the traffic is from repeat sales. There are an enormous number of eBay buyers who will buy something on eBay and when they get their sign and like it, they say, "Can you make me a such and such sign?" And I say, "Well, check out my website at www.texsign.com. Or if it's something I don't already have, I'll tell them to fax me a sketch and I'll see what I can do.

With the eBay user ID "daddyhog" you must be a Harley fan.

Yes. I have three Harley motorcycles.

How about your son?

That's the reason I have three, so he can ride along with me. I recently returned from a motorcycle trip while he stayed back and ran the business.

Did you go online and check things out while you were away on the trip?

Yes. Every night pretty much. Of course I have a cell phone. I called Rick everyday. If we were staying in a motel that had Internet service, I would go in and see how things were going.

Do you think you're addicted to the Internet?

Pretty much. [Laughs.] I can always look to see which checks have cleared the bank and which checks haven't. Then I can get online and check my bank account and my PayPal account then check eBay and check Amazon.

Is most everyone paying by PayPal?

Things have changed. In the 1998 to 2000 time frame almost everybody sent me a check or a money order. And I would say that seventy-five to eighty-five percent of my payments were paper payments. People would send payments to my mailbox. Now it's just the opposite. We used to get eighty money orders a day and now we're getting five. With electronic payments it went from five a day to eighty a day.

And that's mostly through PayPal?

Yes. Mostly through PayPal. People can still call here and use credit cards. We try to take money in whatever form the customer wants to pay. If they want to send me cash, I'll take it. If they want to send me a check, I'll take it. If they want to send me a money order, I'll take it. PayPal is so simple to use now that it's most people's first choice. When my wife and I were out jogging around the college, I was trying to think of how to sell some of these items and I decided to try eBay. We put a half a dozen signs up on eBay and sold some, then sold some more. I remember typing in a search for "parking signs" on eBay and something like fifty parking signs were for sale at that time. I thought, "Well, if I could ever get fifty or seventy-five signs for sale I'd do well." Now I have roughly 1,600 available for purchase on eBay at any given time. Our total number of signs is somewhere close to 6000.

You've designed all the signs yourself?

I've designed almost every one of them.

It's pretty much endless what you can do with artistic ability.

Yes, and we're adding to it everyday. People have tried to copy us. It's no secret. People can see what I have for sale and they see how we have it marketed. There are several people locally who have tried to do this but no one has yet made a living from it.

Well, you could copyright some of those signs that you make yourself.

I have copyrights for every one of them. However, that doesn't necessarily mean that it will protect you. If you ask for a copyright, you'll get it. But they may have given out copyrights of the same sign to various people; it doesn't make any difference. To do well on eBay and pay the bills, you have to do it with volume.

If somebody wants to call you, you'll make the sign and take it to them locally.

Oh yes. In fact, we're working on a project for a private school in town, making banners for the gymnasium wall. There's also a lot of local industry out here. We make a lot of decals and things for instrumentation.

Are the decals silk-screened? How do you make them?

It's all cut vinyl. I looked into doing silk-screens and I may do them one day. Rick and I have discussed it, and the next time we go to a sign show we might end up buying silk-screens.

If someone wanted to get started on eBay, what would be some of your suggestions based on your experience?

[Laughs.] Well, you have to understand that you can sell a bucket of bat guano if you get enough people to look at it. It doesn't matter what you have for sale, somebody will buy it if you can get enough people to look at it. I had a hard time understanding that but there's a truism there.

Well, you get a lot of eyes out there on the Internet.

That's the thing; you get an awful lot of exposure. Who would believe that I could sell "podiatrist parking" signs by the hundreds? Every year we sell 100 parking signs at a podiatrist convention. We'll sell a few in between, but when they have a convention, they either give those signs away or sell them. I think they take them to the convention and either give them away as door prizes or gifts, or sell them to people. Here's another example: we sell what's called a "Space Shuttle Parking" sign. We sell them to The Space Store at NASA. NASA has gift shops that sell them in Texas and California. The trick is to get enough exposure that you can find these people and they come to you wanting signs. That's hard. It really is. In the meantime you have to have good product and you have to keep your costs low. That means when it comes time to buy aluminum, I'll spend $20,000 on aluminum at one time in 4x10 sheets. But the cost per sign is way less than if I was buying a smaller quantity of aluminum. When we buy a cardboard box and ship these things in them we're buying 15,000 boxes at one time. We buy everything in quantity.

Do you have one size of aluminum that's more popular? How many sizes do you have?

Oh, we'll cut it to any size a customer wants. However, unless they ask for something different, it will be 12 by 10. Except for a parking sign, which is 12 by 12.

Do you have any vision for where the Internet's going from here?

Not really. I look at feedback from my buyers. Everyday when I sit down and start making the labels and checking who's paid, I look at their feedback numbers. I'm seeing that we'll get some buyers who have 200 or 300 feedback comments. I've seen their eBay records and they've been on eBay for a long time. I also see that we're still getting a large number of people who have only one or two feedback comments, which indicates that eBay is still growing. I think eBay is still probably in its infancy. I think it's growing exponentially. I would expect that two, three or four years from now it will still be growing because there are so many first time buyers. That hasn't changed since day one.

They seem to be very well managed.

eBay is well managed. I have issues with them. I think they're really arrogant. But if I was the only guy on the block that had an online auctioning company I might be arrogant, too. [Laughs.] You know? They can be very heavy-handed in some of their buyer relations. If you want to do online auctions, eBay's the only place to do them. A case in point: I have a sign that says "Ass Crossing," which has a picture of a donkey. eBay killed the auction and said it was obscene. Then they called me and told me they killed it. At any rate, I got my dictionary out and found that an "ass" is an animal. I spoke with a staff member there and I asked if he'd ever read the Bible. I told him about the guy who killed his enemies with the jawbone of an ass. I didn't think that was obscene. So he thought about it a minute and said, "Okay, we'll back you." We had a bunch of auctions killed that I haven't argued about that probably shouldn't have been killed.

If you want to do online auctions, eBay's the only place to do them.

Did they have the rating system with positive feedback right from the time you started?

Yes. It's absolutely necessary. You need to have that, even though there are some problems with the system. There are people who have given me bad feedback, whom I have tried like the devil to make happy. Like the lady that bought two signs and said she didn't know how to use PayPal. I said, "Well, if you don't want to use PayPal, you can send me a check or money order." She said, "Well, I want to use PayPal, but tell me how to do it." And I said, "I'm not an expert and I can't help you with PayPal, but send me a check or money order and we'll get your signs to you." She gave me negative feedback because she couldn't use PayPal. Well, I didn't think that was fair. People look at that. Feedback is absolutely necessary. I'll buy things from eBay quite often, like equipment and materials, even toys. If those sellers don't take PayPal, I won't buy from them, and if they don't have good feedback I won't buy from them. By "good feedback," I mean to say that a negative rating or two doesn't bother me, but overall it shouldn't total any more than one half or one percent.

Do you know when eBay actually went into existence?

I think it was some time before 1996. I came along in late 1998. Working with eBay is a tough way to make money. It really is. It's like a garage sale. You can have a garage sale and the first weekend you can come out okay, but the second weekend is tougher and the third or fourth or fifth weekend is tougher yet. So the trick is just to find a product that you can sell and that has a pretty good profit margin, which is hard. My son and I have tried selling jump ropes because we're fitness freaks, and at one time jumped rope a lot. If you can imagine, a sixty-year-old man out jumping rope. [Laughs.] But we thought we could build a better jump rope. Of course if we were going to do it we would have to make enough money at it to make it worthwhile.

Unless you just go through traditional channels, like sporting goods stores and the retail route.

Yes. But can you imagine how many jumping ropes we're going to have to sell to make any money? [Laughs.] As far as eBay goes I am satisfied. I didn't understand this until I got involved. Virtually anybody can go out and find a product, turn around and sell it and make a very good living at it. It doesn't matter whether your product is a sign, mowing grass or plumbing. There are worlds and worlds of opportunities out there. Somebody who's willing to work at it and give better service than the next guy is going to find success. It makes no difference what your product is. If you give good service and work hard at it, you'll be okay. At age fifty, nobody wants to take the chance on hiring you regardless of your background. They'd much rather employ a thirty year old than a fifty year old. I'm sure you've found the same thing. So the answer is to go and create your own job. If you look at some people from diverse ethnic groups in Southern California they're successful at being self-employed because they work hard. They go out and create their own jobs.

Right. Well, you're a hard worker and you have a very interesting background. A motorcycle rider, ranger and petroleum engineer. You have had an interesting life!

The Army has worlds of opportunity. I enlisted as a private and, lo and behold, after a couple of years they sent me to Officer Candidate School and offered me a chance to go to college. Years later they offered me a chance to go back and get a Master's and they paid me a salary while I was doing it. There's no reason anybody else can't do the same thing.

Bill Cameta

Knows His Product

Pursuing his interests. You can tell by his energy that Bill Cameta likes what he sells. With over 20 years of marketing experience, Bill has a keen awareness of the importance of customer satisfaction. He ensures this with fair pricing and product knowledge.

Bill, I see that you've been in the retail business for over 20 years now.

Yes, for just over twenty years. We started in 1983.

How did you get into the business? Were you interested in photography?

Before I had my own business, I worked in camera stores. I got started in that around 1973. I moved from Michigan to New York in 1973. I was born in New York and I moved back here in 1973 and got a job at a store called Olden Camera. They were a very big retailer at the time. I believe they are still in business. I had an interest in photography when I was young. I always used to go to different camera stores and wish I could buy stuff. I think it was more of the fact that I liked the equipment more than actually taking pictures, truth be known. Especially since I've been in the business, I don't take many pictures at all. My wife takes a lot of pictures.

Well they are quite a mechanism, aren't they? They're fascinating.

Yes. I'll give you an analogy. Well, it's not really an analogy. My accountant was kidding around the other day and he said, "When I go into Staples it's like sending a kid to a candy store!" He was kidding around, but he obviously meant what he said. I think a lot of people know that feeling you get from places that sell office supplies or stores like Home Depot. You look around, and you say, "Oh man, I must have a use for this stuff!" even though you may not. But I think with cameras it was a little different. It doesn't quite fall in the category, but like you said, they are fascinating mechanisms. Cameras were these really impressive, expensive and mysterious things to me at the time.

Well, digital cameras have changed all that.

Oh, yes.

Were you doing anything on the Internet prior to eBay or is that where you started?

We had a website going back in 1997 or 1998. We had a retail store and we still do in Amityville, about 10 minutes from our offices. That's where we've been for all these years. We had a retail store with walk-in traffic and a photo lab and so on. But we also specialized in used equipment. We still do. We did a tremendous amount of used camera equipment business. Buying, selling and trading. When we first went on the Internet and had our own website, we used it primarily for used equipment. We still have a website, but it's kind of inactive. If you go to our website now it has a list of the used equipment we have in stock, and gives you a link that takes you to our eBay auctions.

How did you drive traffic to your first site?

I used to advertise in a magazine called *Shutterbug*. I don't know if you're familiar with it, but *Shutterbug* is a magazine that started around twenty-five years ago. It specializes in used, collectible kind of equipment. It was designed as a magazine for people who were hobbyists. They got a kick out of the equipment. They liked to try different stuff. They were people who sold all kinds of good used equipment, oddball stuff and junk at a low price. It was like a news print and it kind of caught on, in small circulation. They really became the place where anybody selling used photo equipment would advertise. We were a large advertiser in *Shutterbug* and had been for years. When the Internet came into existence, we had a website and we did a couple of things. In our *Shutterbug* ads we encouraged people to visit the website, which also had equipment. We promoted our website when we sent out their packages. We sent them emails on a regular basis directing them to our website. We did it through *Shutterbug*. We didn't use any other technique.

I looked at your website. You have a very interesting way of ranking the quality of used equipment.

It's a little unique in the sense that it's not a common way to rank used or collectible equipment. That was a variation of the *Shutterbug* ranking system. They had Mint, Mint Minus and Excellent Plus. They had very specific descriptions of what met the criteria for those different descriptors. That was what most early advertisers like me adopted. But I changed it because I felt that the *Shutterbug* wording was too ambiguous. It just really didn't tell the story. A certain category would be 90-95% of the original finish. Now, what does that mean? That 5% of the finish could be completely missing? Or are they trying to say that 90-95% looks brand new and the rest looks something less than brand new? I haven't read them in such a long time, even my own conditions. I remember when I made them, I was trying to convey the idea "this is what you can expect." For those people who want something that's beautiful looking, they'll get something that's at least Mint Minus. If you want something that's nice and clean and serviceable, an Excellent Plus-Plus or Excellent Plus piece is fine. It's not necessarily going to win a beauty contest, but it won't be unattractive. I try to convey to people what they can expect so they're not disappointed.

Have you used the same eBay User ID "cametaauctions" since registering with eBay?

Yes. We have always used "cametaauctions" as our User ID. I think it is important not to change a User ID, so as to not to run the risk of confusing your customers.

Are you selling new and used equipment on eBay?

New equipment is easier to sell and list on eBay because once we create an auction for new equipment we can use it repetitively. Once I have it, I can run it over and over again. I can schedule it to run so that I can sell hundreds of something with the effort of making one auction and running it repeatedly. With a used auction you run into a problem. It's labor intensive to make an auction. At the same time, if it's a used piece of equipment, it's unique. So it means that with some exceptions you have to create a new auction every time you have a different piece of used equipment. It doesn't pay unless you're going to have a piece that's going to bring you substantially more on eBay than it would through some other means of offering it to the public. However, one of my biggest problems is having a sufficient amount of time and manpower to think about and create these auctions. There are ways that I've already thought of to minimize some of that work to list used equipment, but I really haven't implemented it. There are certain ways of making the used auctions somewhat generic, especially for things that you get with some kind of frequency. The four people I have here are completely devoted to just the creation of the auctions. They're busy all the time.

Are you using the Buy-It-Now feature on most of your items?

Yes.

With Buy-It-Now I know you can have a reserve and you can use a gallery photo, but I'm really not up on all their options. Are there some other options that they have?

Without going into the unusual little niches, like Dutch auctions, you have a few choices. You can start the auction at a certain opening price. I consider a true auction as opening your item at a dollar, regardless of the value of the item, with no reserve. Whoever is the highest bidder at the end of the period of time that you're listed for, wins the item. If they get lucky and they get it for two dollars, then they own it for two dollars. As long as you want to have a good reputation and continue listing on eBay, you're obligated to deliver the product. That's the most dangerous, because of the fact that it leaves open the chance that you're not going to get a sufficient amount of money for the item. It's the most appealing kind of auction to a prospective buyer, because they really can get caught up in the idea that, "If I make the highest bid, I can have the item." And that was the way eBay was in the beginning. Mainly it was stuff that was used or collectible, which is still a huge part of their business. Now there's a lot of new stuff being sold. So this kind of auction we do very, very rarely. I'll tend to do it with a used piece of equipment more than I would with a new piece of equipment. If there's demand for something used, this is important to remember. New is a little different in the sense that new is usually readily available. If you have a used piece of equipment that has limited demand, even though it may have high value, somebody could get lucky because of the fact there are not many people competing with them in that particular window of time for the item and there may not be enough bidders to bid the price up. So they can get lucky and steal it. You don't want to be listing valuable things that don't have many people who are going to be interested in it. On the other hand, we just recently sold a couple of very valuable cameras that we've had for a while. One of them was a very early Nikon that was very unique. It went for $10,000. I ran that starting at a dollar with no reserve. It's one of maybe a hundred of its kind in existence. Even if there are only fifty people who are seriously interested and can afford to buy it, those fifty people know that this is one of their few shots to get that camera. They're going to pay whatever they have to. I always figure it's a great way to find the true value of something. If the demand is going to be there to bring it up.

So you actually started that at a dollar with no reserve?

And watched it very carefully!

How many days are your auctions normally?

Three or ten. What I typically do is take an item and make a Buy-It-Now auction in which its starting price and its Buy-It-Now price are identical. Let's just take an example of a digital lens. We have a lens that we sell called the Phoenix 100-400, and we had it listed for $169.95. It lists for $169.95 and the Buy-It-Now is $169.95, so you can't buy it for less than $169.95. We run this type of auction for 10 days. A Buy-It-Now auction where you start and finish at the same price is relatively inexpensive.

You run it for ten days, because you're not creating any sense of urgency to buy. That's the closest I would come to calling it just straight out advertising. You're saying, here's this product that we have. It's $169.95. If you like our price, and you think that we'd be a good place to buy it from, then click the Buy-It-Now button and it's yours. We get to run it for 10 days and if it doesn't sell in those 10 days it's only cost me a couple of dollars. We just keep running it consecutively and sometimes it sells, sometimes it doesn't. On items that I intended to move for volume I'll do it a little differently. I'll start it at one dollar. I'll put a reserve price, and of course nobody can see what the reserve is so nobody knows what it is, and then a Buy-It-Now price. Say you have a dollar starting price and you have a $219 reserve and a $229.95 Buy-It-Now price. There's very little difference between the reserve and the Buy-It-Now. Usually that sells on the basis of somebody just paying the $229.95, knowing that the difference based on past auctions isn't much different than the Buy-It-Now price.

New equipment is easier to sell and list on eBay because once we create an auction for new equipment we can use it repetitively.

If you sell an item at the Buy-It-Now price, that ends the auction. Right?

Yes.

So then you have to re-list it.

Yes. You have to re-list it.

A Dutch auction involves multiple units in the same listing items. How does one work?

I've never taken the time to figure it out. I've tried! (Laughs) A couple times several years ago I tried to figure out the Dutch auction. If I really took the time to do it, the information is there. I knew it wasn't for me and I just said, "The hell with it."

Do you use any kind of an auction management service like AuctionWorks?

No. I don't. We have created our own software for managing our auctions.

Do you send out emails yourself when an auction closes or do you use a service?

Well, I always look at those services as being for companies that don't want to be as hands on. I'll give you an example. Ritz Camera is the largest chain of camera stores in the United States. They're primarily in shopping centers. They mostly do photo finishing, but they also sell cameras. Because there are so many of them, they buy a huge amount of equipment from the manufacturers. They also have a website which they use to sell directly over the Internet. They're a big company with lots of cameras. They run auctions on eBay. Because it's just a small portion of their business, they obviously haven't devoted much in-house to it. Depending on what you want from these auction management companies, they'll do everything from listing the item, creating the auction, and even shipping the item, if I'm not mistaken. The problem is that it's impersonal. In other words, you're not dealing with anybody who's really involved with your business. So I try to do all that stuff in-house.

Do you keep an email database for contacting customers?

We have all that information, but one of the eBay rules is you do not contact the customer directly. You're not supposed to contact people directly through their email address even though we get their email address as a function of running the auctions. With the exception of contacting a winner after the close of an auction, you're never supposed to contact them to solicit anything or talk about any kind of business outside the auction that they won. If you contact these people you're supposed to contact them through eBay using their eBay user ID. In other words, it would be like screening your mail in prison. (Laughs) Theoretically, eBay is making sure offers that are against the rules are not being put forth. Although they probably can't read all the emails, they might have software that picks up key words. Maybe it's just the idea to discourage people from sending things through eBay that they know they shouldn't.

Even if you had to go through eBay it may be beneficial.

Well, the important thing is to remember that it depends on what you're offering. As eBay grows it's becoming a self-policing community of buyers and sellers. Some people are more involved in the community, like me, because obviously this is such an important part of my business. On one hand, the idea is that everyone watches out for everyone else. Theoretically the buyers are watching out for other buyers by leaving feedback that gives buyers an accurate appraisal of who they're considering doing business with. On the other hand, the sellers can also warn people who are doing business with a particular customer that they're not a reliable buyer.

Do you check the buyer's feedback rating?

It's not particularly significant but sometimes you run across buyers who have negative one or negative two feedback, which means that they've bought virtually nothing and that for the couple of transactions that they have made, the seller left them negative feedback. Some sellers will say, "We do not accept bids from anybody with negative feedback." But in reality, it's of little significance.

And they probably aren't going to check anyway.

No. They probably aren't. It goes back to a time when there were a lot of people who had very little feedback. The idea back then was to have a meeting place for people like antique collectors to exchange merchandise with each other. The idea of feedback was more significant in terms of somebody who was a buyer getting negative feedback. I find that watches are a very cliquish kind of category, even though there are tons of people who advertise watches. There's more of a tendency for people to know the buyers and sellers in that category, and a lot of the buyers are also sellers. They're looking to buy and resell at a higher price. Positive feedback is important for a small seller because it's like saying, "I'm not just some guy who does this in my house." He may be, but he's saying, "You can trust me." I'm more concerned with my percentage of positive feedback. We have over 55,000 feedback comments and 99.8 percent of them are positive. I think we have 113 negatives out of 55,000. The bottom line is that as long as I can keep my feedback rating at 99.8, that's fine. If you become lax about your concern for feedback then the percentage of negatives will start to creep up. If you look at high volume sellers, like me, their positive feedback rating percentage is usually in the 98's or low 99's. For all I know, the public regards that as being very high. If someone's looking for an item that many people offer, like photographic equipment or digital cameras, and they're looking at me and they're looking at another seller and they're trying to make a decision of who to buy from, the difference between my 99.8 positive feedback rating versus the other person having a 99.2 positive feedback rating might be the difference in them deciding to purchase from me. Most people probably don't even look at that number. All you can do is try to do your best.

With that many transactions you're going to have glitches here and there. What caused your negative feedback ratings?

It doesn't matter whether you're on eBay, elsewhere on the Internet, or you're face to face with people. There are going to be experiences that are not ideal. Sometimes they're not our fault and sometimes they are our fault. Ironically, those people rarely leave a negative feedback comment. We have a customer service department which we really take seriously. Our customer service people are dedicated to dealing with eBay questions, problems or concerns, and satisfying them. We really take a proactive interest in making sure that the customer is happy. As a result, we tend not to get complaints from people who have legitimate complaints. For example, if we have something for auction and we don't have it in stock then we're not supposed to have put that item up for auction. Because of the volume we sell, we're dependent on getting a consistent flow of merchandise from manufactures. We watch this closely, but sometimes we miscalculate. If it gets past the number and into a negative quantity and they're on back order from the manufacturer, we'll stop running the auction. There may end up being a couple of people who are left in the position of having won an auction, but can't get their merchandise shipped immediately. We call or email them immediately, tell them the situation, apologize and give them options. They don't have to complete the auction if they don't want to, or they can wait and we'll ship it to them later free of shipping charges. We offer certain things like free shipping that is our way of saying, "Hey, we do care. It's up to you to do what you want to do." I acknowledge that there are many people, probably more than the 113, who have given us negative feedback, who have had reason to give us negative feedback, but haven't because of our public relations policies. We sell a lot of equipment overseas and in our auctions we say, "If you are buying outside of the United States, please check with us first so we can determine what the shipping charges will be for this item to your destination." Some people don't check with us. They go ahead and they win the auction, and then they find out the shipping charge. They're surprised at how high it is. So one of the more common negative feedback complaints we get is, "beware of high shipping charges." These are people from overseas who didn't bother checking. Another common one is, "tried to contact them several times, no response." We answer every negative comment. In other words, everybody on eBay has the opportunity to respond to any of the comments that are made about them. So, if somebody makes a negative comment, you can go right into the feedback page and leave a response, so that people will at least hear your side of the story.

Is there any way to change unfair negative feedback comments?

There is a way of getting it removed. There's a company called Square Trade that specializes in this service. If you subscribe to Square Trade as we do, you can set these things up for mediation and there's a fee per transaction. From a cynical standpoint, it's a way for this company to make twenty bucks each time anybody wants to dispute a negative feedback comment. We determine what offer we want to make. Then we will contact Square Trade and say this is what we want to offer this customer as a way of making things right. You make some sort of an offer, like a free memory card, or whatever it might be. Then they contact the customer and ask them whether they will agree to mutually withdraw the negative feedback. If they don't hear from the person within two weeks, they then will take the feedback off, because there was no response from the person. If they do hear from the person, the person will either say, "No, I don't want to make any agreements and I want that feedback to stay," or, "Yes, I'll accept your offer and I'll agree to have the feedback removed." I would say about half the time people agree to have it removed.

Before you started using eBay as a business, were you aware it existed? Did you ever buy or sell personal things on there?

I was aware of it. I never bought or sold anything on it, though. I knew what it was in concept.

Obviously when you made the decision to do this, you said, "I'm going to do it!" And you didn't do it halfway. What kind of an approach do you think people who want to start an eBay business should take in order to succeed?

Well, I really don't know the answer to that. If I was somebody who came from a field other than this, I might be able to answer that question better. When you have your own business, you're really aware of all the different things that contribute to success and failure. Even though you may not know a formula, you know the things that you're constantly taking into consideration. Going onto eBay became just a leap from what I was already doing. You've got price conscious customers and you want them to be satisfied. They want to know that they're buying from a reputable place and they want good service. You've got competition. You kind of apply all the same principles, but you think of them as problem solving. It may look like I rushed into listing things on eBay, but I originally had maybe ten or fifteen auctions. I had no idea what they were going to do. We were managing with our existing staff and there was this extra money. Before we knew it, we had twenty to thirty auctions. We were selling a little bit more and had to hire another person, so it progressed. As it progressed we were monitoring what was going on. If by the time it gets to thirty-five or forty auctions and you see that you're losing money, you either have to figure out a better way to do it, or stop doing it at all. I'm trying to anticipate what's going to go on down the line. I may know what the profit picture looks like today, but I try to protect myself from the worst. That's true of business in general. You have to figure you've got to move forward to at least stay in the same place. If you're static and just try to coast, I don't think your business will work for very long.

Prior to starting on eBay did you surf the Internet?

Very little.

For me eBay is an advertising medium.

So did you have at least some interest in the Internet in the early stages?

I never really did, even after we had a website. My non-business use of the Internet is basically confined to placing an occasional online order or for reference information. Any time I spend on the Internet is business related in terms of looking up one of the companies that supplies me, or looking at orders I have in-house with them, and checking on back orders. By and large I spend very little time on the Internet. I'm too busy. I don't have any time for it. At best I use it occasionally to place an order for something, and more often just for reference. If I want to find something, I'll use the Internet for reference. It's an unbelievable tool. I try to stick with things that I really want to know, as opposed to just surfing around and seeing what's going on.

I hear about the emerging Chinese economy. Is China a future market for you?

I'm not familiar with it. There are so many things that come into play. I don't even know much when it comes to selling to people outside the United States. A lot of it has to do with customs and duties, and what the prices are like for the same product and I don't follow that. I put it out there; I offer it for sale. If somebody from France or England or China thinks that it's a good deal then they'll buy from me. I can't do anything to appeal to them based on lower prices than I can afford to sell. It's really about price. It's also about who you are, and your reputation and so on, but ultimately the main factor is price.

Is there anything else you'd like to add that might be of interest?

I think that eBay offers incredible opportunity for people to go into business for themselves. You don't have to rent a building, you don't have to hire a staff, and you don't have to advertise. For me eBay is an advertising medium. It's a different way of making contact with the customer. But you can start small. You don't have to give up your job. You can do it during your own hours, and you can see where it leads you. I think it's an incredible opportunity for people who have an interest in trying to start their own business. I assume there are thousands of people on eBay who have some kind of small operation in conjunction with a regular job. Or maybe they're retired. You're bound to pick up some extra money, whether it's enough to live on or just to supplement your income. Whether it's enough to be able to have a better lifestyle is another thing. To make eBay your sole source of income is another step. The number one thing is you have to be willing to work and think, work and think, and work and think. I think a lot of people don't realize that in business the most important time you spend on your business is the time you spend thinking about it. You have to execute, but the bottom line is you have to plan. If you don't have a plan, you can't execute it.

That's a very interesting observation. A lot of the time, we're too busy "doing" and we don't have a chance to think.

I agree.

And your wife is taking photographs all the time! (Laughs)

No. She's not. [Laughs.] She's playing with our dog. Truthfully she does a lot of work for the business, but she does it from home. My joke is that in my next life I want to come back as either my dog or my wife! [Laughs.]

That's a good one. I like that.

It has to be part of your makeup. Some people don't have an entrepreneur quality to them. They don't think in those terms. They're not particularly analytical. They should probably do something else. But if a person has that kind of determination and there's nothing really stopping them, then eBay is a land of opportunity. It's a very level playing field; the small guys pay the exact same rates for their auctions as the big guys. I pay the same thing as somebody who wants to sell an old lamp. We both operate on the same fee structure; I get no breaks for being a bigger advertiser. Another thing I want to mention to you that I think is important is whatever you're selling, your relationship with your suppliers is crucial. If you're supplying merchandise or products, you have to get them from somebody and you have to sell them to somebody else. You're a middleman. So much of our profit is not only dependent on the customer paying a price that's profitable, but on our ability to do business with our suppliers in a way that gives us that kind of an advantage as well.

Have you ever met Meg Whitman, the CEO of eBay?

A couple of years ago there was an awards dinner and conference in Las Vegas for the Consumer Electronics Show. eBay gave out seven awards for people who were sellers on eBay in different categories. I was one of the seven, which was very nice. If you go to any of my auctions, you'll see there's a picture of me standing next to Meg Whitman with the award. We got to meet with her for a couple of hours in a private conference room at the Bellagio Hotel in Vegas. The seven of us who won the awards got to ask her questions. I found her to be very impressive and the meeting provided some interesting insight.

Chuck Black

Unique Products Set Him Apart

Looking for products he wants for himself. Chuck Black concentrates on products you can't easily find. He has something for everyone that they would have a hard time finding through traditional sources. Rapport with his suppliers and a keen eye for new sources of products keep Chuck on top.

In looking at your site and your products, it seems you have some merchandise that can't be found anywhere else.

We specialize in unique products and try to find things our customers can't just go to the mall and pick up.

I would think that a person of almost any age would be interested in the items you have on your site. How would you categorize what you sell? On your site you call it pop culture.

Yeah. That's a broad stroke for what we carry, but basically it's an accurate term. Pop culture really deals with anything relating to art, music, movies and television; that's how I sum it up. Some things that are considered pop culture wouldn't fit that definition, and some things, like Harley-Davidson stuff, wouldn't fit it either. But Harley-Davidson is a well-known

77

name. It's a lifestyle brand—I guess that's what I would call the Harley-Davidson stuff I wear.

Do you just keep thinking of other things that might tie in and then add them to the product lines?

Basically that's right. I really carry merchandise that deals with the things that I enjoy and am into. I have only a basic working knowledge of those types of products. It's fun to carry them, and they seem to bring in the same type of customer that I am, I suppose.

I understand you've been involved with eBay for close to five years.

Yeah. I got in before the big push came. So I got in relatively early compared to a lot of the other sellers. But I was actually active on eBay about a year before that as a buyer. Then I discovered I could start selling things on eBay as well.

Where did you come up with the eBay user ID "99volts.com"?

I knew my business was going to "live" online. I had noticed when I purchased items on other websites that I could remember the dot-coms name better when there were numbers in the name. So "99 Volts" doesn't really have any meaning per se; it was just something kind of catchy and memorable. And it seems to work. Everybody always remembers "99 Volts." When we had some computer problems a couple months ago, the repair guy came in and actually said, "99 Volts! I can't believe it. I know about you guys. My son who lives in Sweden bought some items from you off of eBay, and he told me the name of the company he got the stuff from and I remembered it." That was kind of neat. eBay's pretty far-reaching.

How much international business do you do?

We do a pretty good amount of international business. Last time I ran the numbers, about 12 percent of our business was international.

Have you ever thought of using another language on your site, presenting a Japanese translation, for example? Would that be at all useful?

I haven't really thought about it. I know there are tools, like language translators, out there; you can download a program and it will automatically translate a web page for you. But I haven't tried to pursue that. And as far as the website itself I don't try very hard to push it internationally, because then you get into the intricacies of dealing with fraud and credit cards. There's so much credit card fraud, and I'd rather not deal with the hassle of it to be honest with you. In fact on my website I don't allow international customers to purchase with a credit card. If they can go through PayPal I'll allow them to buy that way, because PayPal has done a lot of the legwork as far as fraud for you already. Otherwise, I make them either mail me U.S. dollars, a money order or a bank draft.

Going back to your start with eBay—did you buy some things before you began selling?

Yeah. I found out about eBay as a musician. This was probably '94, '95, maybe '96. I was pretty new to the Internet and was just knocking around some musicians' sites. One of them was discussing this site called eBay that sold this certain brand of guitars. They were normally hard for people to find through the newspaper classifieds or through their local music stores, but you could find them relatively cheap and plentiful on this site called eBay. So I hopped on eBay and sure enough there was this whole slew of interesting stuff. And I purchased a few small things on there, mainly compact discs, to see how it worked. I probably bought ten or fifteen things on there and decided that I was going to try to sell one of my guitars on eBay. I had a semi-rare guitar that was kind of valuable that I had tried to sell locally through the classified ads and at music shows for a couple years, without any luck. It was a real specific item that someone would really have to want to purchase. I placed it on eBay, and there were several bidders—two or three in the United States. A guy in Japan bid on it, but I didn't want to get into shipping overseas because I was new. A guy about two hours away from me in Orlando ended up buying it. I mean, it sold immediately and for a little bit more money than I thought I was going to get. So that's when the light bulb went on, and I realized that eBay was a great marketplace as far as exposure.

It seems like you're using Buy-It-Now quite often on your eBay site. Do you also set a minimum bid?

Yeah. I'll set a minimum bid, and then I'll do a Buy-It-Now at usually a couple bucks more, depending on the item. I don't do any of that reserve stuff. I won't even bid on an item in a reserve auction unless I absolutely have to have it. You don't know where you need to be to even qualify for the item, so I think those reserve auctions are always more aggravating.

Do you use gallery photos—those pictures just next to the descriptions?

I use those sometimes. I used to use them a lot, because eBay promotes them as greatly increasing your sell-through. But then I started doing experiments where I wouldn't do gallery on anything, and my sell-through was maybe just a percentage point lower. So it's not that dramatic a difference. Of course when you get expensive items, like a couple-hundred-dollar item, I think it's a no-brainer. You should have a gallery picture then, because the cost is such a small percentage of your sale, it doesn't hurt you. But for the stuff I sell—which generally ranges in value anywhere from a couple bucks to fifteen, sixteen bucks—if I start getting twenty-five cents added to my auction, that's 30, 40, or 50 percent sometimes of my listing fee. So it all comes down to this: if it would increase my sales by 10, 15 percent, I'd have gallery pictures all the time. But for my stuff, using them hasn't shown to be that important. Besides, I found that a competitive opening price will sell your stuff a lot more than any gallery picture. So that's what I've concentrated on.

Do you use any kind of management software or service to send out emails for you?

I use an End of Auction email in PayPal. PayPal offers an option to where they'll automatically email whatever information you want to send to the buyer. Of course my customers also get the eBay email. But I don't use a specific email service anymore, because I found it actually confused the buyers more than anything. They'd get an email from eBay saying, "Okay, you won." Then a minute or two later they would get one from PayPal saying, "Hey, you won; pay this way." And then maybe the next day, they'd get one from me saying, "Okay you won; send money." And they're like, "All right, I already paid, why do you have to get me for more money?" So I just use PayPal's End of Auction Notification. Now I do use auction management software. I use Seller's Assistant Pro, which is an eBay official product, I guess. But I don't think eBay actually maintains it; a separate company does. The services it offers are pretty nifty. I use it for storing all my ads that I run, because there's a lot of automation in that program. I use it for listing the auctions and storing all the info for each particular auction. And then it also goes and grabs all the buyer input for me. Every morning I run it and import the previous day's sales. Then I import all the information to a custom system that I use online. That system was built for me by a local web developer. He set it up for my particular needs and it includes an automated inventory control system. It's actually really nice. I can go in and I set the levels for when I think a reorder on any item should be made, and the system gets me a daily report on what I need to order, designating the vendors and quantities. Because we started small, I originally did everything on a Microsoft Excel spreadsheet. When I started doing about a hundred sales a week, it got a little bit tough to manage, so I switched over to a Microsoft Access database. I didn't really know how to program it, though, and when I started talking with guys who did computer programming for a living they said I'd be better off using something besides Access.

Can you restock most of your merchandise?

Yeah. I don't sell anything I can't restock, because I have employees and it's costly to deal with items from yard sales and places like that. You can't really do volume with that, unless you spend all day making ads. With my stuff I make an ad one time and I never have to make it again. Whenever I run out of a particular item, I quit running the ad. Whenever I get more in, I just restart the ad. It already lives in the Seller's Assistant Pro

We specialize in unique products and try to find things our customers can't just go to the mall and pick up.

system. So I program it to list the ad on this, this and this day, and to start at this time. Or when I run out I tell the program, "Okay. Don't list anymore until I tell you otherwise."

Do you have a lot of vendors? Do you have to deal with a lot of people?

Yeah. I've got quite a number of vendors. I have sixty or seventy now.

Since you're a musician and have things that are music related, I assume you use your music contacts as leads to sources of merchandise.

Yeah, I've been dealing with music products for a long time. And once you get your foot in the door with a couple of contacts, then you start finding out about other suppliers through trade magazines and sources. So there's a whole wealth of information out there; you just have to dig and find it.

How many items do you have listed out there at one time, would you say?

As far as individual items, I probably have six hundred or so offered at a time. On the better selling items I'll run multiples during the week. I may advertise some every day, or I may run some ads on just Sunday or Thursday. As far as auction numbers, we usually have anywhere from about twelve hundred to a couple thousand auctions running at any one time.

How many days do you run your auctions?

I usually run them for seven days, but I'll run them for three days if the items are popular and sell a lot. With a popular item, you know people don't want to wait. And you can sell-through more during the week. If you offer just a seven-day auction and somebody bids, then you have to wait the full seven days to sell the product. If somebody bids on a three-day auction, or maybe a Buy-It-Now, you can sell at least two times a week. Actually, I offer one-, three-, five-, seven- and ten-day auctions. eBay got smart, though, and started charging a surcharge for the ten-day auctions. There used to be a nice little trick. If you had an item that didn't sell that well, you'd slap it on a ten-day item and you'd only have to run it three times a month and pay the same as you did with a seven-day item. But now I think there's a twenty cent surcharge they charge you for ten-day auctions. They're smart; eBay, they're no dummies. They know what they're doing. They know they've got you. They've probably got more MBAs working there now who have all these formulas on exactly how to maximize profit. And that's how businesses should be run, you know? That's why eBay is so successful. And they're the eight-hundred-pound gorilla. If they actually had a challenger come in that started to take some numbers away from them, you'd see things change as far as that part of it. Now Meg Whitman has come in to maximize shareholder returns, and that's just what she's doing. Like I said, they're the traffic driver. Unless you're Amazon.com, you kind of need eBay if you're online.

Do you have the same products on your website as on eBay, or are there some items on your website that you can't put on eBay?

Well, I have some products on the website that sometimes I choose not to put on eBay just because it actually drives traffic to my website. If people are using search engines, your eBay store will actually turn up in the search engines a lot of times before your website will. So for at least a couple of brands in particular, I actually just leave some merchandise on the website and don't sell it on eBay. Where I may sell one or two items on eBay, I'll have about twenty or thirty different items on my website. Trust me; I'd rather sell on the website than on eBay because it's a lot cheaper.

Are the prices on your website pretty much the same as a Buy-It-Now price on eBay?

Yeah, pretty much; it depends on the product. Actually sometimes it's cheaper on the website, sometimes it's more. As far as the pricing on eBay, I have a formula I use to find out where I maximize my return at different prices. Most of my stuff on the website is pretty consistently priced. Whereas my shirts are $16.99 on my website, on eBay the Buy-It-Now may be $14.99, or it may be $18.99, $19.99, depending on how often people do Buy-It-Now on that item.

Did your educational background help you at all in setting up your online business?

You know, what actually helped me the most is when I was working a regular job before I started selling on eBay. I was in a lead-supervisor position at a local company that manufactured hydraulic valves. They put a lot of responsibility for the success of the product and the departments on the people in charge of them, rather than on the management guys up front. So you learned how to deal with the ordering system and the automated inventory and all that stuff. I learned to use a program that dealt with how many pieces you sell per month and how many you need to have in stock. It also used an inventory management theory called Kanban. It's a Japanese system, where you order at a certain number and then your "re-supply" is supposed to show up the same day you use your last item to maximize your inventory control. That's the type of experience I picked up at the company, and it helped me more than anything in becoming successful online. There's not a lot of brain work in buying and selling things on eBay. If you have a product people want they're going to buy it. But the real trick is when you start doing this for a living. You need to find out how to be very efficient. You're not doing it out of your house anymore, and you have employees. Now you're competing against the guys who are working out of their house and have no overhead.

How many employees do you have now?

Last year we had five, but we became so efficient I cut it down. So it's just me and a female employee, who has been here about a year. She likes it here and I couldn't do it without her. She does a great job.

You mentioned you became more efficient. What changes did you implement to become more efficient?

Basically I became more efficient because eBay is saturated with sellers now. There are a couple of boards on eBay I'm a member of and that I read and take part in. One of them just opened up access based on feedback numbers and all that stuff to the top two hundred sellers on eBay. The Elite, I think is what they call it. Last year, looking at the boards, I noticed that my sales were starting to decline. All the sellers had the same complaint. So around January last year I thought, "Man, I need to get this thing as efficient as possible and start selling more on my website." So that's one reason I had that custom system built and went with the other management programs.

Do you use any sources other than eBay and your website to sell your goods?

Well, for the last three years I had a regular retail store where people could walk in and buy things. I actually just closed that two weeks ago, and we moved to a warehouse-office–type deal. So now it's strictly the online business.

It looks like you've got everything running smoothly, but have you ever used something like AuctionWorks?

I tried Andale for awhile and I used AuctionWorks for a little bit. But, number one, it's so expensive. They want a percentage of your sales and all that kind of thing. So you may end up owing them hundreds, even thousands, of dollars a month whenever you sell at a pretty good volume. And you have to do it their way. If it doesn't offer something you need, then you're stuck. That's why I went with having a custom system built for myself. I've always been pretty good at figuring out, "Okay. I'm here and I need to be there. How can I get there?" I've always had a pretty good knack for figuring out a way to make things work. So I just went to this programmer and said, "Okay. This is where I'm at; this is what I need to be doing. You figure out how to program it and I'll tell you if it works or not." And we'd go back and forth, adjusting the system. With the big professional auction management systems, you can't customize. You have to do it their way, and as I said, sometimes that doesn't work for me. And I tell you, that's a whole challenge in itself— running through all the auction management software to try and find out which one works for you, because there's such a big time-investment. It's a steep learning curve and you're already kind of running full speed. And we literally have thousands of products, and you have to transfer all of them over. If something's screwed up for a week, you're in trouble, because then you're not ordering the things you need to reorder.

Chuck Black

You mentioned you have thousands of products. With such a variety of goods, how would you answer someone asking you cold, "What items do you sell on the Internet?"

I usually tell them I sell pop-culture items. Then I add things like music-related and movie-related t-shirts and gifts. That's probably 75, 80 percent of what we sell. That's the vast majority of it.

Do you use anything like pay-per-click, paying every time somebody clicks into one of your products?

No. I don't. And I see where they offer that on eBay now, as well as on regular websites. In my position on the eBay Elite board, I've read that some of the bigger sellers who have used it say it hasn't really increased their sales and it can get costly. Other sellers claim it hasn't been great for them either.

They're smart; eBay, they're no dummies. They know what they're doing.

I suppose eBay's selling point is the fact that people go there.

Exactly. eBay is basically just a glorified search engine. If you're looking for something to buy you go to eBay instead of Google. And the great thing that eBay has is the feedback system. Otherwise you can go on the Internet and find anything from anyone, but you don't know if they're legit. But with eBay it's all centralized, they've got a good search engine system, and they kind of police it. So people trust buying on eBay.

It sounds like you eased into doing business online. Did you have an elaborate business plan or did you go one step at a time?

I just went one step at a time. Once I sold that guitar on eBay, I started selling a few things here and there. I lost a bunch of weight and even sold some of my clothes that didn't fit me anymore.

What advice would you give someone thinking about starting an Internet business?

Well, in this day and age, especially if you're dealing with eBay-specific goods, I would investigate eBay. I would try and find a product that is either not being sold or that only one or two other people are selling. There's a situation now where eBay's really marketing the selling end–for individuals to have stores–because eBay only makes money on a sale from the seller. They're making a lot more in fees from me now than they were when I was just buying stuff. Their promotion of selling has worked brilliantly, and they've got millions and millions of sellers on there now. Whereas two or three years ago you may have gotten $20 for something, you may get only $8.99 for it now. So, as I said, my advice would be to find a product that not a lot of people are selling and go from there. And the good thing about eBay is you can research their other sellers' last thirty days by doing a completed auction search. You can see how many people are selling the product, how many of this particular item have been on eBay in the last month, and what the going market price is. That's the real secret of eBay success, the thing that's helped me. I've been ahead of the curve on a few trends, and so I've been able to get the products. Have you ever heard of West Coast Choppers? The Discovery Channel has a show called "American Choppers." And right now there's a company on there called Orange County Choppers. But the original company was called West Coast Choppers. I was at a tradeshow in West Las Vegas, and I went by the booth of the company that was making their clothing. I watched their video and I thought, "This is a really neat idea; I think this is going to do well." So I bought a bunch of their products–just kind of taking a chance on them–and sure enough sales exploded. I was the very first one on eBay selling West Coast Chopper products, and as a matter of fact I was selling so much of their merchandise on eBay, the company refused to continue to let me sell things. They quit supplying me because I was outselling their website. They'd actually called me with their attorney on the line and said that they weren't going to sell to me anymore, that I was in competition with their website. Needless to say, I wasn't too happy about that. But that's the thing: if you can figure out what trend is coming up, then you can do relatively well.

Do you keep an email database of everybody who's purchased something from you online?

I do have a database, but I don't really utilize it as far as sending out advertising or other info. That's one thing I've wanted to look into doing, but so far I haven't. Honestly, I really concentrate on eBay. That's where the buyers are. But having a database is something I have in the works, on the back burner. This year I'm going to start doing some advertising in some of the national music magazines to drive more traffic to my website, because it's getting expensive to sell on eBay. Like I said, the prices you get for your products have come down so far and the fees keep going up. It's not like it used to be. I miss the good old days of eBay. Just in February or March they raised the listing fee. I'm dealing with tight margins with the stuff I sell on eBay. Because there are probably ten other sellers on eBay who are selling the same products, it really comes down to price. Buyers don't even seem to care if a seller has reached a poor feedback level. There are certain sellers on there–I can't recall them by name–who have 10 percent negative feedback, which is horrible, but are selling thousands and thousands of items a month. People will continue to buy from them because they price things so cheap. I just can't imagine people bidding on something when they know one out of ten of them is going to be a dissatisfied customer. It's crazy. But even though people are pretty savvy now as far as checking out feedback, they're still looking for a bargain.

Do you have any feel for where Internet sales and marketing are headed?

Well, it's going to continue to grow as far as the Internet in general. People have learned to trust the technology, and there are some really cool, unique products out there. For stuff I use here in the office and at home, I automatically go to eBay and some other online sites to buy things. It's convenient and they ship it right to you. So unless it's something like a car where I need to drive it or a guitar where I want to play it . . . Well, that's not true. I've actually probably bought about twenty guitars on eBay since I've been going to it. One thing about eBay, though, they haven't really drawn in the big companies as sellers. I mean, Disney's on there, but they're just selling old movie props and unique collectibles. I see where the Sharper

Image has jumped in with both feet, but they're selling closeout items. I don't know–eBay wants the big companies, but because of the pricing structure the big companies can't afford to come in. So I don't know what's going to happen on eBay. It's turned into either a bargain site where you're looking to buy something cheap, or a place where you can find a really unique item. I've read a few times where eBay's really killed a lot of the collectibles market. The prices have come way down, and that's what seems to appeal to the rest of the buyers now. Price is number one and unique merchandise is number two. I don't know if eBay's going to reach a point of critical mass where they have to change their price structure. That's the big debate online now with all the big sellers. It's "What happens next?" People were certainly upset with the last pricing increase. Everybody moans and groans every time eBay increases the prices, but I saw a couple of big sellers actually get out of the eBay market last time that happened, in March. This one guy, who had about fifty thousand feedbacks, just disappeared, quit selling. He made a post where he said it was getting too expensive. But as far as e-commerce in general, it's going to continue to grow by leaps and bounds. People have adopted it, especially the young kids. I've got kids who are ten years old buying stuff from me on eBay. It's crazy. So the younger generation has definitely learned to trust the technology and it's just going to get bigger.

What should people do to prepare before they start an Internet business?

Well, number one, they should know how to get around on a computer, obviously. I worked on a few consignment arrangements where people who weren't good with the computer needed someone to sell for them. You can't run a business that way if you're the person paying the consignor because that person's getting all your money. So, number one, you have to have a decent working knowledge of the computer, especially the Internet. And the good thing about working online is you can learn as you go. It's kind of hairy anytime you get onto websites with shopping carts and other unknown procedures. The beauty of eBay is they've made it so easy to sell online that a little kid actually can get on there and learn it in a day or so.

Is there anything that stands out that you wish you could do over again?

Well, I guess the biggest thing was trying to grow too big too fast. Last year I really made an investment in growing the business and bringing in new people. Unfortunately it coincided with the start of the decline of sales on eBay. But I don't know if that was something I could have foreseen. I'm still trying to figure out all of that, because it doesn't seem like I'm the only one who got caught up in it. So I guess if I could do anything differently, I would have waited another year to try and grow things. Then I would have seen that the sales might not be there. But as far as everything else, there's nothing I'd really change. I mean, you learn as you go. And I've been fortunate enough to not overextend myself and get into money trouble.

Is there anything else you can think of you'd like to mention?

Well, I really love what I do. I'll tell you a little story that's kind of funny that shows how my work has changed my life. As I said earlier, I've been doing this full time for about five years. When I first started out, I was entirely on eBay–that's it. I didn't have a website or anything. Even my eBay ID didn't have anything to do with 99 Volts at the time, because I hadn't come up with that. But I saw that I could sell things. For about six months before I started doing this full time, I was making a decent income on the side. The last couple months it got to the point where I was making as much on eBay as I was making at my regular day job. So I quit my job–gave them two-weeks notice, told them I was quitting–and told all my friends that I was going to do this online thing. Well, I just found out a couple months ago that after I told them, a few of them were saying, "He's crazy! He's out of his mind. What a fool!" when I wasn't in the room. And five years later, here I am. I'm running my own business—still. I go to work when I want and go home when I want. Of course I work a lot more hours now than I ever did before, but it's much more rewarding. And that's the main thing: being your own boss. To me it's fun and exciting to make a business successful and figure out new ways to do things. And it's also fun and exciting for me to offer opportunities to my employees. I mean, we have a health insurance plan here, and it's kind of neat. And so to be able to have fun making a living–and not have to clock in 9-to-5 and answer to your boss every day–that's the true beauty of it for me. I even get to bring my little doggie to work.

Do you have a warehouse with an office attached?

It's all included in one. It's a big office. Where I was before, I had a regular storefront, which served as my warehouse out front and the office was enclosed separately. Now we've got everything in one big room and we've got the inventory sectioned out. Our shelves have inventory locations just like any warehouse. We've got the work area to one side of the main office.

How long had you been in business before you said, "I've go to get out of my house and get a separate place to work?"

It was probably about a year when I came to that conclusion. I was working out of my spare bedroom, which is about ten by ten, and I was overrunning the house with everything. I'm one of those people who, if work is in front of me to be done, never stops working. So I was working every day from seven, eight o'clock in the morning till nine, ten, eleven or twelve at night. There are always emails to answer. There are always orders to make. Or there's something else that needs to be done. So that was the key for me. Because I was starting to get burnt out as far as having a peaceful home. A home is supposed to be a place of enjoyment, and for me, it had become a place of work. I had to get my business out of the house. Now my wife and I have an enjoyable home.

Mike Levinson

A Hobby Turned Business

He came through the back door. Mike Levinson used the Internet to find items he wanted to add to his collection of NASCAR die-cast replicas and to sell replicas he no longer wanted. One thing led to another and what had been a hobby turned into a business.

Are you the number one die-cast seller on eBay?

Yes and I don't think there's really a close number two. I watch what other people are doing and I haven't seen anyone else selling similar products in the volume that we sell them. There is one company down in Florida, but they concentrate mainly on NASCAR replicas. We don't sell any NASCAR products, so we're not in competition with each other.

How long have you been involved with eBay?

Since 1998. But I haven't been selling there that long. I never really planned to sell. It just happened by accident and evolved and grew.

Did you keep the same eBay user ID the whole time?

Well, I have a strange username. It's "pdg43y." When I signed onto eBay and picked a username, I had absolutely no intention of selling at all, so I just picked something that was easy for me to remember and had a little personal significance. I was active in Lion's Club International. They have our country divided into districts, and each district has a governor. I was Past District Governor of District 43Y, which is the eastern half of Kentucky. "PDG" is "past district governor." And 43Y is the district I governed. By the time I realized I was developing a business and needed to have a catchy username to get people's attention, I had already developed a big enough clientele as pdg43y that I was afraid to change it. By the way, we put all of our contact information in every eBay auction. It's one of the things we've learned and I don't know why more people don't do this. When I put my phone number in my eBay transactions it made all the difference in the world. I have people calling me all hours of the day and night buying products. Customers will say, "I don't want to go through the hassle of eBay. Can I just call you and order over the phone?"

Your website, Mikes-Racing-and-Diecast.com, is interesting too with your unique punctuation.

It's such a long name that if it all ran together it would be really hard to decipher, so we put the dashes in there to make it a little easier to read. It is a little harder to type in but when most people get there they bookmark it anyway.

So did you start out as a collector initially?

My eighth grade daughter was active in her school's band program at the time I started to get involved with eBay. She was getting ready to go to high school and she wanted a new trumpet. I looked into trumpet prices, which were around $1500. I thought to myself, "I'm not going to spend $1500 for a child who's in the eighth grade and may play two weeks then quit the high school band. She might not like it." It just so happened that the day she and I had that conversation about buying a new trumpet, I read an article in a PC magazine about eBay. It specifically mentioned that eBay sold musical instruments. I thought, "I'll go into eBay and look to see what they have." I ended up buying a used trumpet for $400, which was exactly what she wanted. The case was a little beat but the trumpet was just in mint condition. That was my very first experience buying on eBay. I bought a trumpet and sent some guy I didn't know $400. He would only take cash or a cashier's check, but I was brave enough to send it and take my chances. I didn't get cheated or burned and the guy sent me something that was a bargain. So that got me exposed to eBay. At that time I was a NASCAR fan, as many people in this part of the country are. I had bought and sold some NASCAR die-cast replicas. I got on eBay and I started buying a few cars just for my own collection. So I thought since I had some cars that I didn't want anymore, I could sell them and take that money to buy newer cars that I do want. I started selling a car here and there, and was successful. I thought if I could sell cars, I could sell other things. Like a lot of people on eBay, I started cleaning out closets, emptying the bookshelves, and having an electronic garage sale. It was as much for entertainment as it was for the money.

What type of work were you doing then?

I was a franchise Chrysler dealer for 23 years, from 1973 to 1996. I sold out in 1996 and was semi-retired; I was only 46 years old. Then I bought two Subway restaurants. I didn't really work in the stores, I just watched over them. It might have taken me an hour or two a day per store, and the rest of the time I was free. But I got bored with the inactivity. In 1999 I started looking at eBay seriously. I eventually contacted a NASCAR distributor about buying cars and doing a little business, which was the first time that I ever bought something to resell on eBay. I ordered about $1500 worth of NASCAR replicas at wholesale, and I laid in bed that night thinking, "You damn fool. What are you going to do with $1500 worth of cars?" I was about to call the guy back the next day and cancel my order, when I thought that since I told the guy I was going to buy them, I would pay for them and do something with them. I got the cars in and started selling them on eBay and sold them really quickly. Then I bought more cars and sold them, and just kept selling a little at a time. After it got started, I remember thinking, "If I could build this thing up and sell about $50,000 a year, I could make enough money for it to be worth my while. That would be enough to keep me busy and I think it would be a good goal for the first year." The first full year I was in business I sold about $330,000, and last year it grew to $1.2 million.

Incredible! Have you phased out the NASCAR items and gone into other cars?

Yes. We found other product lines that were more lucrative.

Well, you need to be flexible in any business.

True. I learned my lesson when I was 23 years old and got into the Chrysler business. Chrysler convinced me that my goal in life was to sell cars and the first year I was in business, I sold almost twice as many new cars as the guy who I had bought the dealership from the year before. Of course this was a small town dealership; we didn't have a lot of volume. I looked at the bottom line at the end of the year, and even though I sold a lot more cars, I made less money than he did.

Like a lot of people on eBay, I started cleaning out closets, emptying the bookshelves, and having an electronic garage sale.

Because of the discounts?

Yes. It took me a little bit of time to wise up, but I finally realized that selling cars was a method. It wasn't an objective. The objective was to make money. Selling cars was just the method we used to achieve our objective. That's what we're doing now. Selling cars and selling die-casts is just the method we use to obtain our objective.

I also see you're selling Breyer horses.

Yes. That's an oddball thing in our line. We're located up in the mountains of eastern Kentucky and it's a coal mining region. There are a lot of Caterpillar tractors and heavy equipment up here in the coal mines, and I had a lot of people locally asking me if I could get Caterpillar replicas. So I found a company that distributed them in the United States and I contacted one of their sales reps. I made arrangements with him to buy some of the tractors, and they sold really well. He came back to me later and told me about another product line he wanted me to try. They were Armour die-cast aircraft. He told me they sold really well. Since they were related to what we had been selling, and we hadn't sold aircraft before, I said we would try those and see. When we got them in they sold really well. Two or three months later the same guy came back to me again and said, "I've got another product line I want you to try. Plastic horses." I laughed at him and said, "What do I want with plastic horses? That's not related to what we're doing now at all." He told me they were collectible items. This company's been in business for more than fifty years. They make replicas of real horses. They do Secretariat and Seattle Slew and Roy Rogers' Trigger. Not just off the wall stuff. He told me that there are people out there, adults, who have been collecting these since they were children. There's a lot of money in it. Most of them are limited editions. So he said, "I'll tell you what I'll do. Let me send you 20 horses. You put them up on eBay. If you can't sell them, I'll personally buy them back." I couldn't pass up a good deal like that, so I told him to go ahead. He said he would pick out twenty good ones, and he sent them to me. We put them up on eBay and the first time through, we sold nearly every one of them. You wouldn't believe how many plastic horses we sell. They're not cheap, either. They're about twenty to forty dollars a piece.

How about the Barbie collectibles?

That's another story. As part of the die-cast business we were trying to get Hot Wheel cars. We weren't interested in the little 1:64 scale models; we were looking for the 1:18 scale models. A couple of years ago Mattel held the exclusive license in North America to produce Ferraris and we were interested in getting access to those. I thought I might be able to get hooked up with Mattel and buy them direct, and get them a little cheaper. I called Mattel and talked to a woman there. She said, "Well, we've got a certain minimum order that you have to put in." I think at that time it was maybe $10,000, I'm not sure. And she said, "The other thing is, we don't want you to represent just one product line. If you're going to be a Mattel dealer, we want you to represent all the Mattel lines." I told her I was only interested in the die-cast and she said I should try some of the other lines and see. So I ordered the Hot Wheels and a bunch of Barbie stuff, but just the expensive items like the collector's editions. I didn't want to try and compete with Wal-Mart. We really did well with it. For instance, every year Mattel makes a replica of a Lucy doll. "I Love Lucy." Last summer we sold over 500 of just the Lucy dolls. It was unbelievable. We'd only been selling the Barbie dolls for about a year. Mattel came to us this past December and said, "We've changed our policy on Barbies. You have to sign a written agreement. Now if you buy Barbies from us, you must promise you will not sell them on eBay or any other Internet auction site for one year from the date of release. If we catch you selling them on eBay or any other auction site within one year, we'll revoke your Mattel dealership." I hated to lose the Barbies, but I wasn't going to take a chance on losing the Hot Wheels. We still buy a lot of Hot Wheels and Matchbox models from Mattel.

When you started, you had the experience of looking for a trumpet and then selling some of the items in your garage on eBay. So when you began selling the die-cast products did you handle the whole operation yourself?

When I was still working at my Subway stores, I'd come home in the afternoons and work on eBay. While Nancy and I were watching TV at night we'd pack whatever I had sold on eBay that day into boxes, and the next morning I'd load them in the car and haul them to the post office. We were just doing it ourselves until about six months after we started getting serious. When summer came I hired a high-school kid to come in and just let him pack stuff up for about four hours a day. By having him there to take four or five hours of work away from me, I got to spend a lot more time buying more products, selling more products, and doing the things that I really should have been doing to start with. I could tell when he left that I was going to need somebody full-time. I hired my first full-time employee when he went back to school. Now in addition to myself, I have six full-time employees.

Do you still have the Subways?

Yes. I still have the Subways. Nancy takes care of them.

They've got a good franchise system, don't they?

Yes. They do. I've been happy with Subway.

You probably have a lot of fun watching this business grow!

I tell people that when I go to work, everyday is like Christmas. We get stuff delivered, we open those boxes up, and we never know for sure what we're going to get because everyday we get new products. What else could you ask for than to work in a toy store when you're 54 years old!

How many items do you list at any one time?

We probably have somewhere between 3000 and 4000 different items right now.

And they're all listed?

Yes. We list everything we have.

Is it all Buy-It-Now, with no bidding?

Yes. Because of the type of merchandise we're selling. It's new stuff that's readily available that we want to just turn and earn. It's mostly merchandise that can be bought off the shelf in a lot of different stores. The only way to sell it is by making and setting your own price. It might not be the cheapest price, but between the service that you give and the shipping rates that you charge, people are smart enough to look at the whole thing and realize that as a package it's a pretty good deal.

Once a limited edition is sold out, do you ever have an opportunity to get some of them to resell? Or do you just strictly sell new products?

If we find something that was a limited edition or a distributor who's got some stuff back that he wants to sell, we'll buy them as long as they're still new. We don't do anything in the secondary market. Everything that we sell is brand new. If somebody says to me, "I've got a collection of cars I want to sell," I tell them I don't buy anything like that.

I know very little about management programs that send out emails automatically. Are you using an outside system for that?

Yes, I've looked at all of them. The one I use is by far the best system around. It's a system called AuctionWorks. I was introduced to AuctionWorks when they started up because they decided to find the top 50 sellers on eBay and offer them a special incentive to use their system. They called it their Founders Program, because they looked upon those high sellers to help them found their company. I was one of the people they came to, and I signed up with them. Having a company like AuctionWorks has made all the difference in the world. It's really let the business grow. Anyone who has the intent of trying to be serious about a business on eBay can't spend their time sending emails and doing all the clerical work that has to be done.

What do they actually do?

Well, I'll just lead you all the way through from start to finish, step by step. Let's say I order ten Barbie dolls from Mattel. When those Barbie dolls come in, we either take a picture of them or download a picture. We find an image of them somewhere. Then we go into the AuctionWorks site and we create what we call a template. That consists of the image of the item, the description of the item, and everything that needs to be known about it. For instance: the price, how many we have and the shipping cost. Everything about the item itself. And that's like an inventory record. Then we tell AuctionWorks how many of those we want to launch on eBay, whether we want to do one, two, three or whatever. What AuctionWorks does is it will take that information and send it to eBay. They have a direct connection to eBay and feed that information into eBay almost instantaneously. Along with the template that we have just for that item, they have a master template that shows the layout of all of our auction ads. If you look at our ads, they're all laid out the same way. They all have the same colors and they all have the same boilerplate information in them. The only thing they insert in each ad is the information for that particular item. Everything else is preset. AuctionWorks maintains all of our inventory records. If we've got 4000 items, they've got a template created for each individual item and they maintain the inventory levels. So if we put in ten Barbie dolls to start with, the information that we use for the eBay template also shows up on our website. It's all tied together.

And if you get some more, then that goes in as an addition to the inventory?

Yes. But what happens is when we put those ten in, and tell them to put two up on eBay to sell, AuctionWorks will take those two out of our inventory of ten and reserve those. So that if somebody comes into the website and buys something, we don't sell the same thing twice. It tracks how many we have. If somebody does a Buy-It-Now on one of those then, almost instantaneously, AuctionWorks does two things. One, it will record that sale and it will send that person an email telling them that they've bought it, and it will record the sale in our records. And then almost simultaneously it will list another identical item back up on eBay. So as fast as we sell them, they're put back up there as long as we have inventory available. We never have to re-list again. If we get 100 of something and we tell them we want to sell them one at a time, it will re-list it for us automatically 99 times until they're all gone. So we only have to really put something up for sale one time.

Well, if you have more items, why would you limit what the customer sees to two items?

Because of the listing fees on eBay. Every time you list something they charge you. You put two or three up there at a time, and as people buy them we automatically throw another one up. The more you have up there, the more likely they are to expire without anyone purchasing them.

Does AuctionWorks know you started with ten items?

Yes. We let them know how many items we have.

So they'll know. Okay. And then they'll automatically add two when the first two are gone.

Yes. And then if we order more, then we just go back into the template and we add more. Or if somebody calls us up and buys one item direct, we can go in there and subtract an item. We can manually change the inventory level. That's the first part of it. But the other thing AuctionWorks does is it keeps track of everything that we've sold. As soon as it sells, they will send an email to the buyer and tell them what they've bought, how much they owe, how to pay it, and when it will be shipped. They have all the information they need. Then there's a link in that email that the buyer can go into and click on. It will take them into the AuctionWorks system. And at that point they can tell us if they're going to pay by credit card. They can put their credit card in a secure link there. If they tell AuctionWorks they want to pay by PayPal, it will automatically link them into PayPal. Or they can just print that sheet out and send it with a mail payment. But it will keep track of it for us. If they use a credit card or use PayPal, AuctionWorks will keep track of the payment for us. And then when we ship the item, we just tell AuctionWorks that the order's been shipped, and again it sends an email to the buyer saying, "We've shipped your order today." And then a certain time after that, it will send them another email thanking them for their business. Then it will maintain that record for us in an active record for 90 days. So if there's a question about it or anything comes up later, we can go back and find that order and track it for 90 days and make sure that everything's concluded successfully. Another little service they do for us is we can set the system so that every time somebody files a positive feedback for us, it automatically senses we got that feedback, and usually within seconds, it will turn around and file a feedback for them on the same transaction. So we never have to do any feedback. We rarely ever have to send any emails.

And that pretty much concludes the loop?

Yes.

When you initially started, PayPal was not part of eBay, right?

No. As a matter of fact, PayPal didn't even exist when I started. I can remember when PayPal came along. And it was a free service. You could use it for free and not only did you get to use it for free, but they would pay you five dollars a person for everybody else you could encourage to use it for free.

Before they changed that, we probably made a $1000 to $1,500 referring customers to PayPal, getting them signed up. Because the customer got five dollars and we got five dollars every time somebody signed up. That's really how PayPal got established. You know, it cost them $10 a customer, but it made people come to them and make them sign up because people wanted to get that money. And the sellers, like us, were referring everybody we could to PayPal, getting five bucks a head. You know…you send 200 or 300 people, you can make some money!

So then eBay had something similar, right?

They had a system called Billpoint and it worked about the same. But they came along with Billpoint after they saw that PayPal was successful. And they were a "Johnny Come Lately" and it never did catch on the way PayPal had. PayPal had too much of a head start on them.

So they've eliminated that now?

Yes. When they bought PayPal they just eliminated Billpoint. But we used to have to contend with both systems.

Have you seen a lot of changes in eBay since you first started?

Oh, yes.

What would be some of those major changes?

Well, they used to have a counter on their homepage that would tell you exactly how many items they had available. And I can remember the first time that that counter ever hit a million items. It was the first Christmas that I was ever actually active with eBay. Now, I think they've got four or five million at any one time. I can remember when I started the normal load of transactions on eBay was maybe six or seven hundred thousand transactions at a time. They actually had a counter on the opening page. I don't know if it was accurate, but you could go to the opening page and it would say "There are 716,428 items available on eBay." After they got so big they did away with that.

But the basic program was pretty much the same...did they have a Buy-It-Now feature?

No. They didn't have Buy-It-Now. They didn't have fixed prices. When we started, everything was auctioned.

And they had a reserve option?

Yes. They had a reserve option. To be honest with you we could make more money per item by auctioning those items, but we'd sell a lot fewer items. Given the business we're in, we make our money on volume. I'd rather sell ten cars at 20 bucks a piece than maybe stick one guy and sell a car for 35 bucks. Does that make sense?

Sure. With collectibles, it's got to be a good feeling. Who knows what these things are going to be worth in five or ten years? Everything is limited edition because companies aren't going to make the same thing forever.

No.

Back to the listings. You're using a gallery picture?

You can use a gallery picture, but they charge you extra for that. Really, unless it's something special I don't pay for it, because most people are going to open up your ad and look at the picture and look at your description anyway. A lot of people swear by the gallery. eBay says it increases your sales and increases your profits, but I know that it also increases your expense. I have never used it and I've been successful without it. I may have been more successful if I had. It's just my opinion.

Did they have that originally or is that something they added?

All these features that they have now are stuff I've seen come along through the years. They've added the gallery, and the Buy-It-Now feature, and the fixed price, and the eBay stores, and the highlighted listings and the bold listings. They didn't have anything like that when I started. Subtitles are something that's just come along in the last year.

Where do you see the whole thing going? Do you have any idea where it's headed, or do you have any feel for it?

Well, the feeling I have is more of concern than hope. And the reason I say that is eBay's become well-known enough that the big companies are moving in. I'm afraid that a lot of these big companies are going to cut out the people who are selling their products on eBay and sell them direct. I haven't seen any of my companies do it, but just to give you an example of what could happen...say, where Mattel has told me they don't want me selling Barbies on eBay. What would prevent them from selling those to keep me from doing it? They could potentially say, "We're not going to let anybody else sell Barbies on eBay, but we're going to do it."

Of course that hurts their retail to some extent if they get too successful doing so.

Look at the companies on there now. When I started there was no one there but people selling out of their living room and their garage. And now there are a lot of companies selling on eBay. Of course people look at me and say, "This guy's a great big outfit." But I'm some guy who started selling out of his garage and I've got six employees. We just do a whole lot of work.

Do you do much business on your website?

Just about everything on our website is driven there by eBay. If we didn't have eBay the website by itself wouldn't be feasible. What we get on the website comes from eBay. The way that we'll do that is somebody will buy something on eBay and they get that email from us telling us that they've bought an item. It says, "Click on this link to go to our checkout system." And when they go to that checkout system, on that checkout page it will tell them, "Here are three or four items which are similar to the ones you've bought" or "Do you want to go into our website and see if there's something else you'll like?" Before they actually pay for that item or finish their checkout they can go into the website and pick out more items and add them to the cart. That's a common occurrence.

Are you using pay-per-click to bring people to your website?

We tried that once but without a lot of success. I think maybe it's time to try it again because it's been a while since we did that. Maybe we just caught it in its infancy. They seem to have developed that a little bit better and it's something I had in the back of my mind that we may want to try and do the second half of this year to build up to Christmas. So I would anticipate that we'll be trying that.

But you've got all the same items on the site that you're listing on eBay.

Yes. We list at least one of everything we have on eBay. We don't hold anything back or reserve anything.

If somebody wants to get involved on eBay what should they consider?

They have to be two things. Two traits that not only I have, but that I've seen in other people I've met, who have been successful on eBay. One is you have to be willing and able to work very hard. You have to be a workaholic. If you're not willing just to work you're not going to succeed. And the other thing you have to do is you have to be honest to a fault. If you look at our feedback, we've got over 80,000 positives, we've got about 150 negatives. If you go through and read all 150 of those negatives, you'll see that there are maybe ten or fifteen there that we really deserved. The other things were either misunderstandings or just things we didn't deserve. There's maybe ten or fifteen out of the whole bunch where we really screwed something up royally and we deserved the negative feedback. And I can honestly tell you that there's not a one in there where we've actually screwed somebody intentionally and deserved it. There were times when we just made mistakes and screwed up so bad we really deserved a negative.

What return policy do you have?

We tell people that if they order something and it's damaged in any way or it's not exactly as we represented the product they can send it back for a full refund or exchange it for a different item. If they buy something and it's not damaged and it is exactly as we represented it, but they just got it and they don't really like it or for some reason they just want to send it back, they can send it back and exchange it for any other item we have, and we'll give them full credit for the price of the item. Or if they just want a return, to get their money back, then we charge them a small restocking fee. The only reason for the restocking fee is because if we take the item back and we don't get a little something, then we've lost all the money that we've paid to eBay and to AuctionWorks and we can't get that money back.

Most everybody's paying by PayPal?

It's developed into the majority of our payments. I'd say probably two-thirds of all the money that comes in comes through PayPal.

Do you accept personal checks?

We do accept checks. What we do with checks is, if somebody sends us a check, we hold the order for ten days and ship it out on the eleventh day. People say, "Well it doesn't take ten days for a check to clear." And that's true. A check will usually clear within five days. But if it doesn't clear and it bounces it takes it another five days to come back. So if you get a check that bounces you're going to get it back on the eighth, ninth or tenth day. We get maybe ten or twelve checks a year that'll bounce. The reason we don't get more is because people know that we hold their order.

Is there anything else you'd want to include that we haven't covered?

We haven't talked much about my employees, but I've got some wonderful people who work for me and I tell them constantly they're as much a part of this business as I am. I have GREAT employees, and this business would not be where it is without their contributions.

||||||||||||||||||||||||||||||||||||||||||||||||||||||||||||||||||||||||||||||||

Ravi Sambhwani

A Family Affair

||||||||||||||||||||||||||||||||||||||||||||||||||||||||||||||||||||||||||||||||

Teamwork pays off. Ravi Sambhwani has the advantage of working with his wife and children. He'll be the first to tell you how much his son helped him in launching his initial website. His children allow him to tap in on another generation.

Ravi, your business background is extensive. How long have you been working for yourself?

Well, I've been in business for myself for over 20 years. I owned a pharmacy and then a retail gift store before I started an eBay business five years ago. Since then I have been doing eBay full-time.

Have you had any other business experience?

I do some import-export business with India. I export equipment and import items that I offer to my eBay customers.

Were you born in India?

Yes. I moved to the United States in the early nineties. My family sponsored me. The gift shop I opened was in Los Angeles, and I owned a pharmacy while I lived in India. I switched from medicine to gifts.

Are you a pharmacist?

No. My grandfather was a doctor and he created some medical formulas. I went into that business.

Are you selling similar items on eBay that you were selling in your gift shop?

Yes. I sell everything from gifts and kitchenware to jewelry and furniture and everything in between. I have something for everyone.

Did you just decide to sell on eBay because you don't have to pay rent and put up with all the troubles associated with having a traditional retail outlet?

Yes. I like eBay because there's more flexibility. In a retail store you're stuck there all the time and have to keep regular hours. Even if you don't have a customer in your store you still have to be there. There is very little freedom. You become a slave to you own business.

Where did the name Richie Enterprises come from?

When I was young I used to read a lot of those *Richie Rich* comics. My dream was to be a rich kid and that's where that name Richie came from. I thought it would help me become rich if I name my company Richie Enterprises! [Laughs.] That's why I chose "richieent" as my eBay User ID.

How did you first start using eBay? Do you remember when you were introduced to it?

Yes. I think I saw it on *CNN*. There was a lady who started selling jewelry and she made $100,000 from her apartment. That was about five years ago. I went on eBay and saw many items similar to those I was selling in my retail store.

You have quite a diversified product line. How many products do you have altogether?

Not all my items are listed on eBay right now, but I would say I have about 7000 to 8000 different items. The total number of items in my warehouse is between 30,000 and 50,000. I usually inventory six pieces of one item.

Are most of the items imported?

Yes. Most of them are imported from China.

Was that the same with your gift shop?

Yes. Much the same thing. Most of the items in my gift shop also came from China.

Did you just start putting products from your store on eBay and testing them?

Yes. I tested a couple of items and I started getting bids. Since I started five years ago, there is much more competition and it is hard to get the high prices we got originally. Prices don't get bid up as much as they used to because there are less bidders. The competition has gotten much more intense. This makes it good for buyers but more competitive for sellers.

An item gets the most bids when there are just a few hours left and the item shows up on the first page of a search.

I notice you use the Buy-It-Now feature often.

Yes.

Do you usually have a lower starting bid than the Buy-It-Now price?

Right.

Do you ever use a reserve?

When I purchase items for myself on eBay, I never bid up an item that has a reserve price. My customers don't like reserve pricing either, so I don't use that feature. If I have a totally unique item, and I know it has been retired or discontinued, then I just start the bidding price low and then let it go from there.

Generally your items are priced from around $10 to $50, right?

Yes.

I've seen some of your listings as high as $700.

When my customers go to my eBay store, they see the same thing in the store that I am auctioning. There is a wide price range of items that we sell. We sell some very elegant items that sell for hundreds of dollars. When someone used to step in my retail store, they would buy something and then go. On our eBay store we have a large selection of gifts, collectibles, furniture, etc., which encompass a broad price range, assortment of colors, and different styles so it makes shopping easy.

I didn't notice any gallery photos. Do you use those?

Rarely. Right now I'm paying so much to eBay that if I use the gallery photo feature the fees start adding up. Many times if it's an expensive item I use a gallery photo, but not for the $20-$40 items. I've got 4000 to 5000 items listed at a time, so that's why I stopped using the gallery photo feature.

Are you listing about that many items all the time?

Yes. I always have at least 4000 items listed all the time.

How many days do you normally set your auctions for?

I would say five days is average. Three day auctions are a little too short and seven day auctions are a little too long. Five days is best for me, because it is long enough to get good exposure and short enough so that the auction will close within a reasonable time period. An item gets the most bids when there are just a few hours left and the item shows up on the first page of a search. There's a much higher chance of getting bids when there are only one or two hours left.

What kind of staff do you maintain?

I get a lot of help from my family, from my wife and kids. I've got one person shipping all the time, and another person continuously putting new listings on eBay. There are four or five people other than myself helping with the business.

Do you use any kind of an auction management service?

Oh, I have to. Without one I would not be able to survive. I use Andale because it cuts down a lot of work for me. Anyone who lists a lot of items at a time should use an auction management service, because they do a lot of things to reduce the workload. It's definitely worth it.

What do they actually do for you?

First of all they host an image, so I don't have to pay eBay. Then when an auction ends they automatically send an email to the customer and update customer information on their records. Then they calculate the shipping and sales tax. Andale tells the customer where to send the payment and how to send it. Also Andale shows us what item has sold and when we ship the item it automatically goes from a pending sale status to closed sale status. As soon as we hit one button it triggers three emails. One email indicates that we have shipped the item and a second email indicates that we have posted positive feedback, and a third email is a receipt. We used to have to do that all manually. Andale is also good for payment reminders. After a month, if the customer has not sent payment, then Andale automatically sends them an email.

That's all part of their software?

Yes. I think they're the biggest auction management service company right now and they are also the best. I've looked at a couple of other auction management services but they're not as good as Andale. For me, I think it's worth it.

Are most of the people paying by PayPal?

Yes. Nowadays I would say about 80% pay with PayPal.

And when you first started how was it?

Less than 40% used PayPal then. Mainly we got checks and money orders. We used to check a buyer's feedback. If a customer had at least 200 positive feedback comments, then it was less likely a $10 check will bounce. Over the holidays especially people would be overspending or stretched out, and a check might be likely to bounce for even a $10 item. Right now most of our customers use PayPal so we don't worry about checks bouncing.

Does that management service program check anything about feedbacks or is that just up to you?

No. They don't. We have to make a decision to ship it or not. Usually we check feedback and if they pay by check we wait ten days or two weeks, and then ship it out as soon as the payment has cleared.

How about international sales? Do you ship overseas?

We do ship a lot to Canada, Australia and the UK. We also ship to Japan, Germany and France. For us these are the top six countries outside of the U.S.

Are there local warehouses that supply you imported items so that you don't have to wait a long time for delivery?

Yes. We import and we buy locally as well. We do both.

Can you order small quantities of an item?

If I'm importing from China I have to import a large quantity –at least 100 pieces. Sometimes a Chinese company will make us order 3000-5000 items at a time. If I am able to buy the item locally it's an advantage. I can buy as few as three items when I buy locally. It's always better to buy locally because if the item doesn't sell you're only stuck with a few items. If you import and it doesn't sell, you're stuck with a lot of items.

Is your website linked from eBay?

No. It's not connected. eBay doesn't allow it.

I only see ceramic items on your website.

I have people designing my website right now. I think in a month's time we'll have a lot more items up. I have somebody in India setting up my website and it's much cheaper to get it done there than here. Soon I should have about 1000 items on my website.

Will they be different than the items on eBay?

Most of them items will be same.

How do you bring people into that site? Do you advertise in some way?

Right now I'm not advertising because I don't have many items uploaded to my website. I only advertise by sending emails to existing customers. We target collectors, people who like particular themes and to customers who have already purchased a certain category of item.

Do you have a separate email list you use other than your eBay customer list?

No. They are all customers from my eBay sales. Whenever a customer buys through eBay we have a database that stores their information. Andale does that, also. They have a database of all my customers. If a new item comes in I can email my customers and introduce them to the new item and offer them a special price.

Do responses have to go through the eBay system?

Yes, through eBay.

Do you plan on using a pay-per-click service on your website?

No. I don't use that. I plan to use banner ads. Once I have a lot of items on my site then I'll start advertising with banner ads.

Before you started selling on eBay were you familiar with the Internet at all?

No. I was not. I didn't know the difference between a mouse and a keypad. My son knew everything, so he set me up and posted my items. I started learning from my son. It was with my son's help that I got started. Youngsters today know everything; with them it is much easier and much less expensive to get started.

If you didn't have your son to help you set up your website, you would of had to of paid somebody big bucks.

Yes. It's expensive to hire people, especially for technical work. In those days it was a booming time for website designers and high tech people. They charged a lot more then than now. So by using my son it was a good, inexpensive start for me.

What is your vision for the future of the Internet?

I think it's still growing and a lot more people are getting into it. Everyday I get new customers who tell me that this is the first time they're buying something online or on eBay. I sell a lot of kitchen items, so a lot of my customers are women who have not been buying online. From their emails I learn they are buying online for the first time. I would say eBay is getting a lot more popular in smaller cities and towns. We ship a lot of our items to these small towns.

Well, that's interesting.

In fact, I hardly have any customers in New York City, Los Angeles, San Francisco, or Miami. I hardly ship anything to these cities although there are millions of people living there. I've got a lot more customers in small towns in remote areas. It's amazing. They will email me saying, "I've been looking for a cow breadbox for the last two years and I could not find it in any store…and then I found you!" In fact, most of my sales are coming from these less populated areas.

So you are profiling your customer base?

Yes. I reply to the emails and I know exactly where I'm shipping my items. Sometimes I'm amazed by the names of the cities. That's why I know a lot of people are buying from small towns and cities. We can tell from shipping. Also we can tell if a customer is in a remote area by checking shipping charges. When UPS is shipping, if an address or a residence is located in a main city they don't charge extra. If they ship to a remote area they charge $1.50 extra. If the address is in the same city but it's a residential address, rather than a business address, UPS will charge us $2.50 extra. By analyzing freight charges we get to know if the city is big or not.

So that additional $2.50 charge to a residence versus a business comes right out of your bottom line.

Yes. That's why I started shipping USPS. USPS does not differentiate between deliveries to business and residential addresses.

You have to deliver items shipped by USPS to the Post Office, right?

They will pick up at my location, but they charge a $15 flat fee. The Post Office is close by so I take the shipments to them myself.

A lot of things have probably changed on eBay since you started.

Oh yes. They're always changing their fee schedule, so we have to stay on top of that all the time in order to get the most for our money. For example, if I had a lamp in four colors they used to allow us to show these four colors in one listing. Now they want us to list the item in four separate listings. They also increased their listing fees. Twice they have increased listing fees, once from 25 cents to 30 cents and then again to 35 cents.

Do they give you much warning when they're going to raise fees?

Usually they give us one month's notice.

If someone wants to start a business on eBay what should they be considering?

Well, on eBay you have to be very different. There are so many people selling on eBay. Even the big companies are selling, like Sears, Dell and IBM. The more unique an item you have, the better chance you will have of selling it and succeeding. It was not like that on eBay five years back. Today you have to come out with a very unique item or you need to be a direct importer. If you import directly then your costs go down and you can sell your imported item for less. Others might be buying locally, but if you're importing you have an advantage over pricing.

Is there any advice you have for people interested in starting an eBay business? Is there any information you think is critical to know?

I've seen a lot of sellers who don't know what they are doing. If they list an item for $25 instead of $24.99 they would have paid double the fees, so for an extra penny they are losing 60 cents. People new to eBay have to research all the options and charges. I am always surprised at how many new people make foolish mistakes that cost them money. If somebody's selling 10 items or 20 items a day and they have not done the research then they can lose a lot of money by not optimizing their listing. 30-50 cents extra doesn't sound like much, but it becomes a lot when you add up all the listings that you make in a month. I also think that the photographs should be really good. If the picture's not good then people don't feel like taking a second glance, and they just go to the next item.

Because you're not using gallery photos, your descriptions have to be thorough.

Oh yes. Key words are very important. If I'm selling an item, say a lighthouse lamp, I do a listing for "lighthouse," one word. Then I use "light" and then "house," two words. Somebody might search for "light' and then "house" would be a second word. I also do "lighthouses." So at least my item has a better chance of coming up on the search, because I've got all three different ways a person can search for lighthouse. In fact, eBay called me and the only suggestion they could give me was that I should also use colors like red or yellow in the description or title. They also complimented me for taking advantage of all the different key words. On eBay you can search only on titles or you can search both titles and description. If you don't have space in the title for two or three different key words, you can list them in the description. Key words are important. So is a good photo.

Do you have an option as to different colors you can use on your descriptions?

Yes. I used to not use colors, but now I do because it makes the description stand out. Especially if I want to give some importance to a particular key word, my price or the shipping information. It attracts attention.

What's the standard color?

I use blue as a standard color, but you can use any color. There's no charge for HTML or color or script.

Does the whole description have to be the same color?

No. People use different colors. I think that looks too gaudy when you mix colors and it becomes hard to read. A lot of people use capital letters in the title. If you see two listings and one is in capital letters and the other one is in regular letters, it is much easier to read the one that is not in capital letters. I use only the first letter in upper case and all others in lower cases.

Did eBay contact you because you do a lot of business?

Yes. They were contacting all the "PowerSellers." "PowerSellers" have their own account managers and special customer service because we are selling a lot more.

Everyday I get new customers who tell me that this is the first time they're buying something online or on eBay.

So you have better communication with them.

Right. We have direct phone numbers for the account managers.

Is there anything else you can think of that would be important that you would like to add?

Prompt communication with customers is important, because now everybody wants instant answers. Everybody wants everything instantly, nowadays. If you don't reply fast in sending an email then buyers feel that your service is not good. I guess they are used to everything fast. If somebody sends an email they expect a fast reply. That's also key for any online business. If a customer wants to send money and you don't reply quickly, they get worried about sending you money.

Do you still have the capability to email the customer yourself even though the auction management service is automatically sending out emails?

We still have direct email correspondence with our customers. Normally there's no need to email. If they win the auction they go on the site, enter their address and authorize a payment, and the product is shipped. Even if my description says where to send a money order they often email me about it. When I send them the information they seem to be comfortable sending me the money and doing business with me.

People like to know there's a real person that they can communicate with. What's your return policy?

My return policy is if you don't like the item or the color you can send it back and we will refund you the cost of the item, but not the shipping. Once we ship the order, UPS or the Post Office will not refund us our shipping costs. That's why we only refund the cost of the item.

So you basically have a total refund policy with the exception of the shipping cost.

Yes. We'll hardly get any returns, because it's hard for a customer to repack the item and go to the post office or go to UPS and stand in a line. Sometimes even if they don't like it or the size is too big, they still keep it or they give it away as a gift. The more accurately you describe an item the less chance there is of it being returned.

Rich Horowitz

It's Rock and Roll

He likes to go to work. Ever since Rich Horowitz can remember he has loved rock and roll. He collected records as a kid, learned to play guitar, and owned records shops. Everything he does is centered around rock and roll. Today he represents the art of rock and roll legends. He truly lives his passion.

I know you've been actively involved with business on the Internet for many years. What led up to your interest in having a web-based business?

It started out as an extension of the record business. I had been in the record business for 25 years. It seemed like a logical extension for me in terms of a way to market and sell all types of out-of-print records, including rarities that we only had one copy of, and things that we'd accumulated quantities of. We amassed so much inventory just from being in business for so long and buying record collections constantly. We found that we had thousands and thousands of out-of-print records. As for selling on the Internet, there are only so many records you can sell through physical retail locations. We thought the Internet would be a great way to expand that market. That was the original impetus for building Off The Record Vinyl, which was our first website. Before we uploaded the site, we put in about 15,000 out-of-print records.

You catalogued all those different records and titles? That must have been a lot of work!

Every single record. It was visually graded. There's some standardized grading terminology that record collectors use and that's what we used when we graded them. Every single record was looked at and graded visually - both the record and the jacket. Not only was that information put onto the website, but these elements were also added: the artist, the title, an LP, a single, or an EP. Each of those items was differentiated on the website with a configuration, whatever it was. We added any necessary comments to each particular item. For instance, we'd include information about whether the record was a mono or a stereo release, whether it happened to be a particularly rare cover, and whether there was writing on the cover or on the labels. We had a whole system of putting comments into the database, in addition to the basic information that any record collector would want. It was hours and hours of work! It ended up taking over a year.

How did you calculate your start-up costs for your Internet-related business project?

Well, we got bids from several web developers to see what costs would be involved in developing the site. That was step one. We already had 60,000 records in stock that were paid for. Our initial main hump was just getting the development of the site done. We budgeted a little bit for advertising, but our main goal initially was to get the site up and running, and then let it evolve.

It's interesting. With the Internet, once it's up there, it's all electronic, and it costs virtually nothing.

Right. You just have to pay for maintenance. It wasn't a huge budgeting scenario. We thought, "Let's get some bids. Let's get the best deal on the best site, and just spend it." The entire inventory was already taken care of.

Wonderful. Did you have any feel for how you were going to get people to come to your site?

We did. Initially we tried a few different things. We ran print ads in record collector magazines because we felt that was an obvious place to advertise. We ran print ads in *Goldmine, Discoveries, Record Collector, Record Convention News* and places like that where record collectors would see the ads. We also tried some banner ads. We linked up with some other websites. We tried various things to get people to come to the site. I think print advertising worked pretty well for us because it was a very specific group of people we were targeting. We advertised in record collecting publications because the product was for record collectors.

Okay. What books and articles did you refer to for advice before you started your business?

I didn't.

You didn't?

No, because I had already been in business for 25 years. I opened my first store in 1974.

You had years of experience running a business...

Yes.

So you learned the most as you were going along?

Absolutely. You try things to see if it works. If it works you keep going along that path. If it doesn't, you change tack.

That was during a time period when the Internet was new to most people, wasn't it?

Yes. It was. Interestingly enough, many record collectors that we talked to weren't even online! The longer we had the site online, the more that changed.

Interesting! They knew where to go, but they couldn't get there!

Right! They'd have to go to a library. We did also have an 800 number, in addition to the website. In our print ads, we wrote, "If you have specific questions, call our 800 number," which a lot of record collectors did.

Where did you go from there? What was the next step?

The next step? Well, we started listing things on eBay. We found that some of the stuff would sell really well. At that point we started adding posters to what we were selling. Initially we used eBay as a way to drive traffic to the website. Now eBay frowns on that. They don't like you to do that. But at the time, early on, in the description of the items we would say, "By the way, if you like what you see here, check out our website." We would have 100, 150 items up at any given time on eBay. That helped to drive some initial traffic to the website.

Would that be similar to what now is called a store on eBay?

Yes, though we never actually created a store on eBay. We would just have listings. Of course, now you can have an eBay store. It's a good way to sell products for people who have many quantities of various items.

Are most of your items either one of a kind or limited quantities?

That was the case when we first started. We would sell out-of-print records, and we would buy collections from radio stations or individuals. We now sell posters that we are able to have quantities of. At eBay, when you're listing the only record that you have of a particular artist, you photograph the single or the LP, put it up online, write your description, and grade it. That's very labor intensive. We now have a stable of posters—really, really cool posters that you don't necessarily see anywhere else. We're able to photograph them once, do the description once, list them once, and then once they sell or don't sell, simply re-list them. It's a huge time saver.

These poster quantities, there is a limit to them. It's not an ongoing, limitless supply that's available. Correct?

Correct. Some of them are really beautiful, hand-pulled serigraphs. Some are very beautifully licensed reproductions of posters from the 1960's. There is a limit, but we're able to re-list on a regular basis with that kind of product.

Are you doing anything with the photography in your inventory on the Internet or eBay?

Yes. We are. We do have a retail location in New York City. What we have in our gallery there is exclusive because we are the publishers of that photography. No one else can get that photography unless we wholesale it. At this point we're not doing that. The retail location is really the primary source of revenue. When people come into the gallery, however, if they look at a photo and say, "I'm not sure whether I'm ready to buy. I really like that Keith Richards, I really like that Mick Jagger, and I really like that Doors. I just can't make up my mind today. Do you guys have a website?" Then we give them all the information. They're able to go to the website, look at the photographs again (because all the photographs are online), and make a final decision. Customers can either purchase online because it is an e-commerce site, or call our 800 number and order the photograph of their choice. Frequently we find that with the fine art photography, the low end is $400. The prices range from $400 to $2,500. We find that customers really like to talk to somebody, get information about art, maybe hear the story behind the photograph, and get information about the limited editions before purchasing. They ask, "How are these photographs made? Are they made from the original negatives? Are they hand-signed?" All the kind of information that people who are spending hundreds of dollars would like to know, but can't necessarily get on the website. Or perhaps if they read about it on the website, maybe they're still not clear about it. Having the 800 number available helps expedite the sale.

How did you educate yourself on running an auction or online store?

Trial and error! It's really not any different than retail sales, as long as you know the price of the items that you're trying to sell. We learned a few minor tricks. We tended not to put reserves on items unless they were just really, really rare, because if the item is worth more than you put it up for, it typically reaches that price anyway. People kind of like the excitement of thinking, "Oh, you know, I may get it. Nope, he may get it. Nope, I may get it!" and so on. Online stuff isn't that much different than retail, other than the fact that you don't have to face the people day to day. There are people who like to take advantage of you, by bidding on items and not paying, so we developed systems to keep track of that and make sure that people are paying you in a timely manner. If they're not, then you get out the bidder alerts. If they don't respond to that, then you have to request money back from eBay, because you've paid a percentage of that sale. Whether or not those people pay, you're paying eBay that money. If the people don't pay you, you've still got to get your money back from eBay. They make you jump through a few hoops and file a few forms to do that, but it's worth doing because if people are bidding and not paying you, they're probably doing it to several other people. If eBay gets three notifications that these people are not paying, then they bump them off eBay. It is possible to re-register under a different user ID, but at least they have to do something. You do end up getting your money back from the percentage that you paid. Those are the kinds of systems you need to put into place.

It's really not any different than retail sales, as long as you know the price of the items you're trying to sell.

You carry the Henry Diltz photographs. Do you have the exclusive right to market those?

Yes. Everything.

Everything that he has? There must be thousands of those.

His archive really consists of about 600,000 photos. That's not all only rock and roll stuff. He has got an amazing archive with some very historically significant photos. Some are album covers, some are not. He did the Doors' Morrison Hotel album cover. He did the very first Crosby, Stills & Nash cover. These are both very iconic album covers in rock and roll history.

It's Rock and Roll

What really sets Henry apart from the other photographers is the intimacy of his work. Any photographer can stand in the audience and shoot guys on stage playing, and many people have done that. But Henry started out as a musician in the late 1950's and early 1960's, and he befriended many of these people. That's what made him so different. He was real big in the folk scene. That's when he initially met Stephen Stills, Neil Young, Graham Nash and The Lovin' Spoonful. So, because he was "friend first, photographer second," they had a very different feeling about Henry being around. They were very casual and he captured it. Henry's quote was always, "I'm the Jane Goodall of rock photographers!" He would just kind of sit on the sidelines and pretend he wasn't there. Because of that style, he created such intimate photos. That's very much unlike the photographer who comes in and says, "Okay, turn on the lights! You guys stand over here, we're going to do a group shot," and the photo ends up being very orchestrated. That is not Henry's style at all.

Do you sell multiples of the same photo?

We do. They're limited editions.

Okay. So there is a set number of photos.

Absolutely. We do three different sized photos. We start with 11 x 14 photos, which are all hand-signed by Henry. Those are open editions and the price is commensurate with that. They're $400 to $500. You can get an iconic photo, hand-signed by one of the world's greatest rock photographers. If you want something a little more special, we do 16 x 20 photos. Those are limited to 275 worldwide. Those range from $800 to $1,000. We do a very small edition. 20 x 24 is the size of the photo, and we do it in editions of 100 worldwide. Those are typically about $1,400.

So collectors would pick a series for purchase?

Yes. Typically people who just want to start getting involved in photography collecting and can't afford something larger are very happy with the 11 x 14's. People who have already established a bit of a photography collection really like the idea of the limited editions.

If they're numbered, say from 1 through 275, are the lower numbers more valuable than the higher numbers?

They're not. They're not more, or less, valuable. What is most important is how many are left in the edition, not the particular number that you have. Number 1 is not any more valuable than number 275. That top number just identifies your print number. There are a lot of galleries that sell lower numbers as being more valuable. We don't really buy into that philosophy because the editions are all created, they're all identical, and number 1 is exactly the same as number 275. When the edition is first created and released, that's the opening price of the photo. Once that edition's gone, it's gone. The only way to then acquire that photograph is to find collectors that have it that are interested in selling it. It's called the secondary market. That's where all fine art moves to once the publisher has sold out of the edition.

Are you involved in that part of it at all, or have you been involved in the secondary market?

Yes. In addition to Henry's photography, I'm one of two people in the country that tours with the John Lennon artwork. So I've been very involved in the secondary market as far as the Lennon art is concerned, because we have clients who are looking for pieces. Once the estate runs out of certain editions, the only way we can find them is on the secondary market.

In the Lennon collection, are they limited as well?

Yes. They're all limited.

And about how many would there be in a series?

With a typical John Lennon artwork that's hand-signed by John, the series would be limited to 345. Those were done in 1969. So those have been sold out for years. The only way to find those is from collectors. Typically, the Lennon art is an edition of 300. There are song lyrics that Yoko has released that are hand-pulled serigraphs. They're taken right from John's composition notebooks and they're limited to one thousand worldwide. So, yes, those are limited. In some cases they sell out very quickly. The prices appreciate considerably on the Lennon art.

It's Rock and Roll

How did you get connected with the John Lennon Estate?

I started out as a collector. I was always aware of the Bag One lithographs. I knew when they came out, and I was in high school at the time. I couldn't really afford the Lennon art, but I always wanted it. In the mid-1980's, I was able to get a complete set of John Lennon's lithographs. It's a set of 15 lithographs and each one is hand-signed by John. But there was one little piece of the set I was missing. It was just a big vinyl bag that all of the lithographs were sold in. I had to have that bag to complete my collection. I happened to be up in Laguna Beach and went into a gallery where they had the bag. I started talking to the gallery owner and mentioned to him that I had some record stores in San Diego, and I thought it would be kind of a cool idea if we partnered and did a Lennon show at one of my record stores. Initially he thought it was kind of a crazy idea, because being a fine art gallery owner, he'd never done anything in a record store. But he reluctantly agreed, and we put together a John Lennon exhibit at my store in 1990. We ended up having thousands of people come for it. People just loved it. And I think the fact that it was in a record store was great, because it kind of disarms people. I think certain galleries have a tendency to be intimidating, but this was exciting. It totally tied in! I mean, it was rock and roll!

So where did it lead from there?

The show was very successful and we decided we were going to try and do something together. It took us a little while to figure it out, but we decided we would go to another city and try just a couple of day exhibits. We picked Seattle. We went up to Seattle, and Yoko's assistant came to the show. She had heard we were doing this exhibit and she wanted to see how we were doing it and if it was representing the estate well. She wanted to make sure everything was on the up and up. She came to Seattle, and we really hit it off. We had a great meeting with her. She liked the way we presented the artwork and we ended up meeting with her a couple more times after that show. She said to us, "You know, there's nobody in the country that is really touring with this. We have a couple of galleries that have some representation of the artwork, but nobody's really taking this on the road. If you guys are willing to do it, we'll give you the full support of the estate." Of course we were thrilled. We love doing the exhibit.

The person in Laguna—he had his own collection?

Yes. He had just a few pieces in his gallery.

Are you strictly doing the traveling exhibit? Are you featuring anything on the Internet at all?

We do have a website. It is primarily an informational site. I think buying fine art on the Internet works, but it works only to a point. I think when you're in a room filled with the artwork and the music playing and 500 people, it has much more of an emotional impact than if you're just sitting at your home online and you happen to pull it up and say, "Oh, that's a nice John Lennon piece." I think the shows are really critical to the success of the website. People do come to the Lennon shows. They come into our built gallery. Sometimes they buy later from the site. They go back to the site, get information, and then come back to the gallery, or come back to the show. I think all of the components are important. To have just a website wouldn't necessarily work for us, but it's a huge part of the puzzle. I think when you do the shows, have the website, and have the toll-free number; all of those things go a long way in making people feel comfortable making those kinds of purchases from you. The two websites that we have are LennonArt.com and Artchives.com. At LennonArt.com, we have the history of our tour and our tour schedule. We talk about the artwork and the limited editions. We have current pricing. It's all the information that people are looking to see. The other website, Artchives.com, is the site that has all the Henry Diltz photography.

How did you meet Henry, and how did that relationship come about?

We had a mutual friend in New York City who did clearances for music videos and for licensing. For example, let's say you had a video clip of the Rolling Stones and you wanted to air it on VH1. You can't just take that clip and air it. You have to get licensed from the Rolling Stones, from the record companies, and from the publisher. A woman that I knew in New York did that. She knew that I had been doing the Lennon exhibit for awhile. Henry had used her to get clearances for the documentary that we did about him called "Under the Covers." So when Henry was looking to do something with his archive, he contacted this mutual friend in New York for suggestions.

She said, "Well you should talk to Rich Horowitz, because he's been doing a similar kind of thing with the Lennon art." So Henry's manager called me, and we chatted about what I had been doing and what they were interested in. We had a few meetings, and they liked the idea of creating limited editions and doing a tour. We ended up becoming partners.

Well, that's a great story. Your passion for the art led to the alliance, as did having that show in your record shop. That led to you getting the relationship with the Lennon art.

Absolutely. That led to the relationship with Henry.

You learn as you go, and what works, works.

And all this stemmed from your collecting records as a kid. Which reminds me, didn't you sell most of your record collection recently?

I did. I sold everything except my personal collection, which is still pretty extensive. I had the stores for 25 years. I sold the last store a year and a half ago, and at that point, I still had 60,000 records in a warehouse. I wanted to focus on the gallery and on the Diltz photography, and I just wasn't interested in spreading out my time too thin. Last December, I sold all of the remaining vinyl that I had in the warehouse. Now we're focusing on growing the gallery. We want to open up several more galleries. We've proven the concept, and now we're just looking to grow it. That's where I want to put my effort.

On the Lennon art website, there are two of you who basically do these tours, correct?

Correct. And we pretty much split the country up so that we don't overlap with the cities. What we typically do is create a list of cities that we are planning on incorporating into our tour over the next year. We submit that list to Yoko's assistant, and she looks at it and approves it. Then we just make sure we don't overlap each other.

As far as the website goes, do you advertise each other's showings? Other like-minded galleries? What about the Lennon Estate?

People see information about our shows only at LennonArt. com. As for the estate, they do their own promotion. They focus mainly on the east coast and the south.

It looks like you've got quite a nice blend of marketing tools here. When you got started on the Internet with your original website, did you work with any graphic artists?

Oh yeah, we had web designers working on it.

Did you have a budget?

Absolutely. We went to them and said, "Here's what we need. We need a database that'll hold X amount of units. We have to make sure it's totally searchable, so if someone wants to look up an artist or a title or search by 45 or EP or LP, it's done." We had a number of meetings to talk about the nuts and bolts of the website and what we needed, and then they did the graphics around that and incorporated the technical aspect into the design.

When you started, you were starting out of your home with that business?

Correct.

Seeing that you have an office now, would you suggest people start out a business working from home at first?

It depends on your personality. If you're the kind of person who can walk out of an office in your home at night and shut the door and call it a day, it's a nice thing. But sometimes those lines blur. Sometimes you feel like you're always at work. You need to decide whether having a home office is a good thing or a bad thing.

How did you find these web designers?

We were referred to them. I knew a woman in the art business who was actually one of the first people to do fine art online and she had a very, very successful business. She actually referred me to these people. We met with them and liked them. We liked their design eye.

It seems like because of the software that we have today, doing web design was a bigger deal then than it is now.

Oh, it was a very big deal then, and it was not cheap to have websites designed. It took months and months to get the thing to a point where we actually went live with it. It was a very slow and expensive process.

Of course with 15,000 items in your database to begin with and having to catalog each one of them, that's quite a chore.

It was. It was very labor intensive.

Okay. Did you do any researching in regard to your competition?

Yes, we did. We looked at other websites. We looked at other people. We asked the age-old question, "How do you get listed on the search engines?" That sort of thing. We found out there wasn't a deep, dark secret. You just have to have good web designers. The record business actually was very competitive, even early on. There were a lot of vinyl retailers' websites. Of course you like to think that your design is superior and that your product is superior, even that your overall service is superior. But the truth of the matter is there was a lot of competition. There were a lot of record dealers online then.

How do you handle returns?

Our policy has always been, "If you're not happy with anything, you're going to get a full refund." I think when you're buying something sight unseen, it's important to make people feel comfortable. And so our policy has always been, "If you don't like what you get, send it back. We will give you your money back." Interestingly enough, we can probably count our returns on one hand. We've always been very, very conservative in our record grading and our tendency was always, "If it's between grades, use the lower grade," as opposed to a lot of record dealers who will use the upper grade. We've had so many very happy customers through the years and very, very few unhappy people and very few returns.

Do you have a reserve price on these items?

No. On the website we didn't. Everything was featured at a fixed price.

So it was a Buy-It-Now kind of thing?

Yes. It was just a price. You look up The Beatles and here it is: "Meet the Beatles," a reissue, ten bucks. You want it, you buy it. If you want the original mono pressing, it's a hundred and fifty. The only time we use a reserve on eBay is if it's a particularly unique or rare item that you don't want to let go of at any price, because it's something that you're not going to see again or you're not going to see for a long time. So in those cases, we use reserves.

So a starting bid is generally the lowest amount that you would want to sell the item for?

Exactly. We try and start most of our records right around the $10 price range.

So if you get to $10, you know that you're either going to get that, or more?

Oh, yes. It says right on there, "You're the high bidder." Whatever that opening bid is, you're the current high bidder, and if no one else bids that's what you get it for.

Have you ever looked into any of these auction management services that handle a lot of detail?

No. We haven't. We use a service that eBay has, software that they have called Seller's Assistant Pro, which is a way to manage all the items that you have.

And that works out pretty well?

Yes. That works out really well.

Did you start right out with that?

No. We didn't start out with that. We started out just by doing individual listings, and upgraded to their next software which was called Turbo Lister. Then we upgraded to Seller's Assistant Pro. It's actually a subscription software that they give you for $15 a month or something like that. It's a good management tool.

Do you have any way to encourage repeat customers with your eBay program?

The best way we encourage them is by making sure they're really happy with their product. Our shipping is very fast. When people win something and pay for it, they get it very quickly. The quality is also good. I think our overall customer service ensures loyalty. If you email us a question, we respond quickly and I think people like that. We treat it like a business as opposed to a hobby.

Since you don't have a store, would they go in with your eBay user ID, "artchives2", to see what else you had?

Yes.

That almost works like a store.

Yes. It does. We have six or seven thousand pieces of feedback, with only six negative responses.

That's great! That's a lot of volume there!

Yes. 99.9 percent positive feedback. When people look at our feedback on eBay, they see that our feedback is near perfect. You can feature a little page that says "About Me", and we have that there. Basically we say, "Hey we've been doing this on eBay for six years; We've been in the business for 25 years. We know what we're doing, and we do a good job."

Excellent. As for your internal computer systems (as opposed to eBay), do you have any backup systems in case of technical or unforeseen difficulties?

We have two different computers in the office, and we have both computers backed up onto DVD.

Do you do that on a regular basis?

Yes.

Are they stored in a fireproof safe, or anything to that extent?

No. We're not that paranoid about it.

What are your suggestions to those just starting an Internet business?

Know your business. Whatever business you're doing, make sure you know it. I think that's the best advice. Don't get involved in something that you don't know anything about.

What specific mindset do you think has been of greatest benefit to your business?

I think you just say, "Hey, I can do that!" The interest has to be there first. That is critical to being successful. Again it's knowing your industry and having interest and passion for it. Then just say, "I think I'm going to try that whether it works or not." I think trying it's the most important thing.

The World Wide Web can be almost overwhelming with information. Can you suggest how a person can sort through this maze to most efficiently educate themselves about the options they have to market on the Internet-from auctions to creating their own store?

The kinds of things that I've tried have been marginally successful. Early on, we were trying to get listed on the search engines and things like that. We had some success with that, but it's a real hit or miss kind of thing. It depends on how good your web developers are. It seems like the search engines are always changing their logarithms and their criteria for how they search for things. It's almost like you have to have a full-time tech person who's working on that all the time. Even then, you're not guaranteed that you're going end up in the Top Ten searches for things. So it's pretty much just trial and error. You learn as you go, and what works, works.

What are some of the biggest mistakes you've made?

I haven't made any really big mistakes. I guess one of the mistakes was not spending the time to add products to our website on a regular basis. This is because the volume wasn't high on our Internet site for the records. I'm not talking about eBay, just our website. That's probably the biggest mistake you can make: not keeping your site fresh. I think that, with record collectors in particular, it's very important to update regularly. They're looking on your site constantly. For example, say you're a Beatles collector and you go to my website and say, "Let's see. I got that, got that, got that. Nothing really on the site I'm looking for right now, but I'll check back in a week." Let's say you check back in a week. Those same records are still there. Then you check back a week later and they're still there. Every time you check back the site is stagnant. Soon you will stop checking in with us. I didn't really keep the site fresh. At that time, I felt it was more cost-effective to put resources into putting things up on eBay where there were a huge amount of eyeballs looking at them and stuff was selling, as opposed to spending six or eight hours a day putting things on my website when sales weren't really commensurate with that.

What particular day stands out that really provided you with everything you want your business to be? Was there a specific day where you said, "Hey, everything's gelling today?"

No. It was always kind of a constant evolution. There were certainly a couple of really exciting days when things sold for crazy prices. We once sold a 45 for $2,600! Those are always fun and exciting, but it isn't the way business happens normally.

Wow! What did you think the high bid would be?

Well, you know, that's the weird thing about it! I researched everything I could on this 45 and I found out no information about it before and after I listed it. I was going through boxes of records from a radio station collection that I had bought. I pulled out this single that looked kind of weird, and it was a label I didn't recognize. It was a group I didn't recognize, but it had a cool look to it. I couldn't find out any information. It wasn't in any of the price guides. I called a couple of friends of mine who had written books on obscure singles and I just couldn't get any information. So I put the single up for $9.99. About four days into it, I guess, it reached about 100 bucks. And at that point we were all saying, "Wow! Well, if it's 100 bucks on eBay it's probably worth at least a couple hundred." Within the last hour it shot up to over a thousand! There were two different people bidding on it and they drove it up to 2,600 bucks!

Incredible.

It was incredible.

Do you remember who the artist was?

Yes. It was The Magnetics and the label was the Sable label.

And it was in excellent condition?

Oh, it was in great condition.

It wasn't signed or anything?

No. It wasn't signed.

That was a good day!

That was a great day!

Did they pay by PayPal?

No. They actually FedEx'ed us money at the time. It was a buyer from the U.K.

On the other side of the coin, is there any day that stands out where everything seemed to go wrong?

Oh, yes. There are always days like that. Those are pretty consistent. I think when you're in business you just have to roll with it. Whether it's a customer complaint that you need to deal with, or payroll service issues, or framers, or, someone not signing photos correctly. It was always something.

How much does the difficulty in packaging and shipping costs figure into whether or not you want to sell a product?

Shipping costs never figure into it, because the customer always pays for that.

But the packaging costs ... some things are a lot harder to handle.

Not really. We've pretty much streamlined what we do, and at this point, we're only handling 45s, posters and rare photographs. So we've got all the quantities of all the material that we need right here at the warehouse. It's a pretty simple procedure.

If you find that you're overstocked in a particular product, what methods have you found to be the best to create the quick sales and reduce the inventory?

That's not really applicable to us, because we don't sell quantities of stuff. Usually we just have "ones" of certain records. And with the fine art photography, the editions are fairly limited. So we're never really faced with an overstock issue.

Do you have a system or guidelines for sending your existing customers follow-up promotional emails?

We don't do emails. We do direct mail.

Have you tried emailing?

No. With what we're doing now, which is the fine art photography and the gallery, we feel letters and/or postcards work a lot better. If we release a new image, we have a postcard printed up. If we have some kind of a special event going on, we try to send all of our collector's letters. I think it's a lot more personal than an email blast.

You've got a lot more attention, and they've got something in their hands.

Right. And there's just so much junk email that's going around. It's very frustrating because I get so many every day. I tend to shy away from doing big email blasts.

Are you doing anything to try to flag search engines to get them to pick your site?

Not really. We have the information printed on our business cards. If people call, that's fine too. With what we're selling the most of right now, which is the rock and roll photographs, we find it's a very emotional kind of sale. People who come into the gallery are hearing the music and seeing over a hundred photographs all around. They're talking to people and hearing the stories of the photographs. If they decide at that moment they don't want to buy, then the Internet becomes very effective for us. They can go back to the site and say, "Well, I was debating between these two different Doors photos, but I think I'm going to take that one." It's much more of an after-the-fact scenario.

Right. When you started using eBay, did you enter those items yourself? Or did you have an employee do it?

I started off by myself and eventually I got some help. Now my employees are an important part of my business. I give them flexibility to be creative and to come up with their own ideas, which not only benefits me, but allows them to utilize their individual talents. I trust them explicitly, and I believe they trust me.

You learned how to do it and then you passed that information on.

Right.

Do you see your sales expanding internationally at all?

We do a lot of international sales, but it's not because of the Internet. It's because of the gallery in New York. It has to do with having a gallery in an amazing location where people from all over the world come to visit us. We end up shipping a lot of merchandise internationally.

And as far as sending out newsletters, it's all pretty much going through the regular U.S. mail?

Yes.

So are you filtering out your past customers so as not to mix them with your current customers?

No. We just mail all the customers.

Sort of a mass mailing?

Yes. If we're doing some type of special event in New York. For example, if Henry's doing a slideshow, then we would send mail to our New York, New Jersey and Connecticut clients only. If it's something where we're talking about something new that we're doing or a new release and we want to let our clients know about it, then we would mail everybody.

Understood. So what are your thoughts about the future of Internet marketing?

Of marketing or the Internet as a sales tool?

As a sales tool.

I think it's a fantastic sales tool.

Do you see any technology that's going to make it more flexible?

Interesting question. I don't know. I'm not a tech guy, but I'm sure that they'll be coming up with new things, like fraud prevention, although it's pretty safe right now. I'm sure they'll come up with new and more exciting ways to market products.

What do you think Internet marketing will be like in five years or ten years?

I think no matter what happens it's going to be very exciting. It's an amazing technology.

Rob Yeremian

A Straight Shooter

He paid his dues. It is almost as if Rob Yeremian is at an intersection where emerging vehicles are crossing at the same time. He experienced early on in college the value of the Internet as a communication haven even before there were websites. He used email to communicate back and forth with his professors. After college Rob gave up a year of his time to work without pay to learn a business. When eBay became established Rob knew this offered a great opportunity for him to capitalize on his knowledge and experience. He has the ability to regroup and is able to remain focused. His business model is based on a blend of a traditional retail outlet and the Internet. The last thing Rob wants to convey is the illusion of "getting rich quick." He is a realist and tells it as he sees it.

I see that you've been on eBay since 1998. Did you have experience on the Internet before that?

I have been involved in computers and telecommunications since the mid-eighties. Back when we used a Commodore 64, we had modems and had to go through the phone lines. I've been telecommunicating more than half my life. When I was around thirteen I was already connecting to electronic bulletin board systems, and I used to run my own. I was in college at the time when email was created, when there were no websites on the Internet yet. Email first started popping up when I was an Economics major in college during the early nineties. I graduated from the University of Rhode Island. Teachers would email students homework assignments, and you could contact them via email if you had any questions. The whole thing gained momentum because universities needed to communicate with one another.

So you go way back before most people had ever heard of the Internet.

I was definitely one of the first who took advantage of the fact that computers could communicate through modems and phone lines.

Have you owned more than one retail outlet?

This is the fourth retail outlet I've owned over the years.

Did you sell collectibles in the other stores?

Yes.

So you already had retail experience before eBay came along.

I had a pretty large store prior to the existence of eBay. I sold the store just before discovering eBay in 1998. I sold my store in August of 1998. When I found out about eBay in October of 1998, it killed me because I would have been able to make a ton of money if I had kept that store. The items I was selling were comic books and other collectibles that were selling like hot cakes on eBay. Had I known about eBay, I never would have sold that store. Unfortunately, it just happened that way.

Was your entire inventory sold with the store?

All of it went with the store and I had to start from scratch again.

But you had contacts, right?

Oh yes.

A Straight Shooter

What did you do after you sold your store?

When I started again in 1998 I was just working from home and living with some friends after moving back from Los Angeles. I moved to Los Angeles after selling my store. I was going to start from scratch again out in Los Angeles, but I decided to come back to Rhode Island. I started doing eBay from home and ended up needing more space, so I rented a house. It just was growing too quickly and I ran out of room and needed more space. I opened up a store and started hiring a few employees. Eventually we were doing so much on eBay that it wasn't worth keeping the retail store open. I closed the retail store and moved into a warehouse. I hired more guys and outgrew that warehouse in a year, then moved into a bigger warehouse, and hired more people. I did that for awhile, but it just got to be too much work. It wasn't paying off because the economy got bad. We entered a recession, September 11th happened, and there was a general change in collectors' tastes. The business wasn't working anymore at that level. I was doing 2000 auctions a week, and I had ten full-time employees. My warehouse seemed like the size of a city block. It wasn't paying off. I liquidated everything.

How did you liquidate it?

I sold the inventory in every way imaginable.

Were you primarily selling comic books?

I was selling comic books, toys and collectibles in general.

Were those the kind of things you collected as a kid?

My interest is in making money. I'll sell anything as long as I can make money and it's legal. I just ended up concentrating on collectibles and comics because it's easy for me to buy them at reasonable prices and sell them at a profitable level. Every year eBay has their eBay Live function. For the first couple of years they paid for me to fly to these events. I'd be sitting around with all these PowerSellers in our special lounge. People always end up talking about the same thing, mainly what they're selling. Nine out of ten PowerSellers sell the same exact things. They either sell computers or jewelry. When I told them I sell comics and toys they just couldn't believe it. They don't understand how I can buy and sell in such volume. I don't mind telling

145

people what I do, because I know nobody can really replicate my success. Someone would need twenty years of experience under their belt to do what I do.

It takes experience, time and energy.

Yes. I have key contacts that I have accumulated over a lifetime. I don't even knock myself out buying inventory. It just walks in my door practically everyday.

Tell me about your website "thetimecapsule.com". I see that you don't sell anything on your site.

The site offers people information about my retail store and a link to my eBay store. It's just to give people a general idea about what I have to offer. It's just there so people can get to know me. We do all our sales either on eBay or in my retail store. I've had websites developed over the years. They're generally a waste of time.

Eventually we were doing so much on eBay that it wasn't worth keeping the retail store open.

Is it because it's almost impossible to drive traffic into them?

To have a successful website with the kind of volume I want I'd have to invest tens of thousands of dollars. You know, it may cost $50,000 to launch a site to create lots of business. It's just not going to work if you invest less. Plus you have to devote so much time in keeping and updating the inventory. It's just not worth it.

Do you have employees in your store?

Yes, but the employees I have are all for eBay. None of them work inside the retail store. They all list or ship.

Are you using any kind of an auction management service?

We've been using AuctionHelper for many years now. They're not the biggest, but they offer more services than a lot of the others. I've been with them for so long and I've done so much business with them, that I feel I get special treatment. When I have a problem they generally take care of it rather quickly. I know with some of the other companies if you have a problem they may not get back to you until 24 hours, 48 hours or even longer.

I notice that on eBay you use the gallery photo feature for your items.

I'm glad you noticed because it shows that you're paying attention. Until I started this current incarnation of my business, I never ran gallery photos. When I was doing 2000 auctions a week it was an added cost that I didn't think I needed. We sell a lot of one-of-a-kind items now, so it is worth using the gallery photo feature. If you're selling the same item week after week that extra quarter it costs for a gallery photo is not going to make any difference. When you're selling one-of-a-kind and high-end items it's definitely worth the money.

Do you just start with an opening bid and no reserve? Do your items ever have a Buy-It-Now option?

Well, 99 percent of the time they don't. Most of our items are $9.99 with no reserve, and no Buy-It-Now option. We let the customers dictate what the selling price will be. Whether it sells for ten dollars or one thousand dollars, we let the buyers decide. I don't like it when people start prices higher because that defeats the whole auction process. If you want $400 for something and you start the price at $400 it's not really an auction. It's a set sale. I find that people who start their prices high have a low sell-through rate. The sell-through rate is the biggest problem all eBay sellers have.

When would you use a reserve?

The only times I use a reserve is when I'm selling a consignment item for somebody, and they've made it very clear that they don't want to sell it for less than a certain price. Or if there's an item that I know I could probably sell in my store for a certain amount of money, but know I can sell faster on eBay. If I have an item that I know I can sell myself for $500 I might not be able to sell it for two months in my store. If I put this item on eBay I know that if I include a reserve of $500, I won't get less than $500. If I don't get the $500, it's not the end of the world, because I'll sell it in the store. It just may take longer. But if I can sell it on eBay and get the $500 now rather than wait a month or two, I'm ahead.

How many days do you normally set your auctions for?

Seven days. Because ten days is too long, people just don't pay attention and they loose interest. If you run three day auctions you don't get as much exposure. I find seven days to be the ideal amount of time. I will start some auctions at five days to get more auctions running and time it so that they end at the same time as some of my seven day auctions. Sometimes this makes things more efficient. There are only so many hours in the day. Employees can only get so much done.

Do you do much international business?

Yes. We have a fair amount. I don't really know what percentages, but we sell quite a bit to international customers through eBay.

Is most everybody paying by PayPal now?

I would say the bulk of international and domestic people pay with PayPal.

What other method would they use?

They also use international money orders, checks or BidPay.

What happened to your website?

Well, let me tell you what happened with the website. It's pretty simple. At one point eBay realized they were losing sales by letting people directly link from the auction listings to their websites. The website I had developed was huge. We had thousands of items. We were doing incredible business. We were using eBay mostly as advertising to attract people to our website. When they cut that out, it effectively killed our website as well as thousands of other people's websites. We used eBay as much for advertising to bring traffic to our website, as we did for the actual sales that we created on eBay. When eBay said we couldn't link to our websites anymore that effectively killed our website.

Have you tried pay-per-click advertising?

I've tried it. It doesn't drive enough business. When you pay Google or Yahoo to be at the top of their listings it is probably one of the only things that will pay off. I'm just not interested in getting heavily involved in advertising programs.

Do you think a lot of your business comes from people who click into your eBay store via your auction listings?

No. The only reason why I have the eBay store is just to help people navigate through the auctions I'm running. I think the eBay store works well if you have gallery images for everything. When someone finds an item I'm selling, many of them will go and look to see what else I'm selling. They can click into my eBay store, go to a subcategory that's related to what they've already clicked, and see little gallery images of whatever else I'm selling in that category. It may or may not increase sales, but it definitely helps people navigate to my other related items. That's the only reason why I have the store.

Where do you see the future of eBay?

There's definitely always more that can be done, but it's almost going to be overkill. They will have too many options for people. I thought Buy-It-Now was a great feature and the stores definitely have some validity as well. It's tough to say. I like the simplistic nature of the way I do things and it seems to work well enough. They can add as many features as they want. I'm just not going to get involved with all these additional things.

Have you ever really been surprised at how much someone bids for an item?

Of course. Anybody who's done this long enough is going to get little surprises. Then you have equally bad surprises, like when the bid gets high and the winner doesn't pay for the item. I almost don't like seeing bidding go too high because I instinctively know that I may not get paid.

Can you go back and sell the item to the next highest bidder?

They have added that feature in the last year or so. Before that it was a big pain. Sometimes you'll see in people's auctions where they demand payment in three, five or seven days. That's not a good business practice, especially if it's through the mail. We end up letting people go sometimes twenty-one days or longer until we decide they need to pay. By the time we go to email the next highest bidder, they're not interested anymore. They've already moved on to other things. So you just have to re-list items from scratch and let the chips fall where they may.

Do you use some kind of an assembly line for writing the descriptions, taking photos, doing uploading, etc?

That's exactly what we do. Everybody has a specific job. It's tough getting good employees to write good auctions. I have to settle for whoever's reliable, because the fact of the matter is anybody who's good is going to start doing it for themselves. I've had a lot of employees over the years doing eBay for me, half of them end up leaving and going off and doing it on their own after learning from working with me.

---

eBay is not a get-rich-quick scheme.

Have some of them done well on their own?

None of them have done extremely well. They all do enough business to make it worth their while.

Do you have any suggestions for someone who wants to start a part-time or full-time business on eBay?

Well, nobody should start doing eBay full-time right from the start. People should just start doing a few auctions here and there, because you can't count on a regular income from eBay. Every week is a new journey and you hope you make enough sales to cover all your expenses. If someone just quits their job and decides they're just going to sell on eBay full-time, they're inevitably going to fail. People are better off just doing it in their free time and as they get more comfortable doing it, they can eventually get into it full-time. Nobody has any business becoming a full-time eBay player right from the start. The biggest problem that everyone has is finding products to sell at a profit level. If you ever go to any of the eBay Live events, you'll get to see firsthand what the bulk of people are really like and what kind of people they are. eBay has seminars about different closeout websites and encourage people to buy inventory to resell on eBay. The problem is when you find some good products on these closeout sites, fifty other people are going to find them as well. If you don't control the market on at least one of these items, you're always going to run into someone who's going to undercut you. In this case it's the auction buyer who wins with eBay. If some guy's selling cell phones, there's always going to be someone who is willing to sell them for a little bit less and make the sale. Especially the guy who has a full-time job and is only selling part-time, he's happy making a much smaller profit margin. That's why I'll never get into selling mass merchandise; the profit level is too low. I have the luxury of being able to do what I do, but most people don't. I went to some of these seminars and witnessed the eBay sellers. They're all sitting there writing pages and pages of notes trying to figure out where to find more products. That's what stops most people from doing this full-time. Even the guys that go out to flea markets and yard sales, they're only going to find a limited amount of stuff they're going to be able to sell at a profitable level.

Well, that's good advice for people. Is there anything else that you'd like to mention?

Like I said, start small. Don't get in over your head. You shouldn't partake in any business venture until you know what you're doing. I've probably bought out fifty different businesses that have failed. The biggest reason why every one of these businesses failed is because the people who started these businesses didn't have enough of an idea about what they were doing and what they were getting into. If you take the guy who drives a truck for a living, but has always really liked comic books or liked toys- this guy gets hurt and gets an insurance settlement and thinks this would be a great opportunity for him to open a business and do something he really loves. But if you open up a business with no prior business experience, you're probably going to fail. I've seen it happen with eBay. I've seen a lot of people who quit their jobs and threw tons of money into buying inventory, computers, getting spaces and hiring people. Many of them failed, because they just didn't have practical business experience. I'm not going to go and open up a pizza place, if I don't have any experience selling pizzas or making pizzas. So what I try to tell people is, don't get involved in something you don't have enough knowledge about. Prior to opening up my first comic book business back in 1993, I went and worked for another store for a full year for free. I did that to learn the ins and outs of what it took to own a comic book store, so I wouldn't make all the stupid mistakes that I knew were possible to make. The year that I spent working at that guy's store will pay me dividends for the rest of my life. There's also another thing I'd like to add and this is very important. eBay is not a get-rich-quick scheme. If people are starting a business on eBay thinking they're going to make a ton of money all at once, they need to know that isn't true. It's just like any other business. It's a job just like any other job. If you're going to do this full-time you have to treat it like a full-time job. You have to put the hours in. There are times when I think it's not worth all the time and effort, but then I think of the alternative—working for other people. I'd rather work twelve hours for myself than work eight hours for somebody else.

It's a huge benefit not to have to punch a time clock and take orders from someone else.

I had the dream business. I had ten people. We were doing an incredible volume. But at the end of every week, after paying all my utilities, paying my wages, paying my taxes, paying for inventory, I wasn't making any money! That's why I had to close down the warehouse and lay everybody off, liquidate everything and start from scratch. It got to a point where all I was doing was good deeds for other people by keeping them employed. That wasn't helping me buy a new car, helping me buy a house, or helping me pay my bills. That's life. Sometimes you just have to call it quits. Luckily I didn't get in so far over my head that I couldn't recover and start up again. I've seen it happen to plenty of other people. My last comment is to be sure to think things through before overextending. Success will come but give it time.

Mike Ray

One Door Closed, Another Door Opened

A heartbreaking experience. The corporate policy of a manufacturer prohibited Mike Ray from marketing their product line on the Internet. Mike had to discontinue a business that he had exerted a major effort to launch. His positive attitude and desire to succeed again, coupled with his Internet experience, helped him to launch another booming business.

Were you in the shoe business before you got involved with the Internet?

No. It was actually the other way around. I previously launched an online site that marketed Sprint PCS mobile phones. It was founded in 1999. Unfortunately, the Sprint PCS corporate policy on independent Internet retailers choked off that business. As that was winding down, I had a friend in the wholesale shoe business in Boston who mentioned I should try to sell some footwear online. One thing led to another and we started on eBay as an experiment. Subsequently, we kept growing and growing and growing. That was about three years ago.

Did you have any Internet experience prior to launching your Sprint PCS site?

That was the first. I jumped on the bucking bronco.

How did you bring people into that site? What method of advertising or promoting did you use?

At that time there was a company by the name of Goto.com. I believe they're currently named Overture.com. They were seemingly the most successful "pay for placement" keyword search program. We were constantly fighting to be number one under "cell phone" and "Sprint PCS". I also paid a programmer a decent chunk of money to naturally embed a code in our website to get us into the top of web searches for certain keywords. Instead of trying to drive people to our site to buy a cell phone, it seemed a lot easier to attract those who were already looking for a cell phone by triggering our link through key word searches.

Were you in the cell phone business prior to launching this?

No. I'm essentially a serial entrepreneur. I started mowing lawns when I was ten. I started a car detailing business at seventeen and a ticket brokering business for sporting events and concerts when I was in college. After college I was involved in a number of small business startups including marketing titanium mountain bike components that were made in Russia. The initial draw of the Internet for me was the ability to reach potential customers all over the world, not just in my local area. It was the ability to reach out and touch somebody clear across the country or clear across the world that attracted me to the Internet.

Is international business a factor for you?

Currently it's not. People constantly ask us about that because a majority of our business is done on eBay. Some of the most frugal individuals in the world are our customers. It's the nature of the eBay customer to be frugal. People in other countries are constantly asking us to misrepresent the value of the product we're sending them and seem to get offended when we don't. We decided that it works just as well for us to say that we do not ship out of the United States, so we're not put in that position.

Was eBay the first approach that you took when you marketed the shoes?

Yes. I didn't have a website. I had been essentially burned after working a tremendous amount of time and spending a tremendous amount of money on building the website to sell Sprint PCS phones. eBay was a viable option for testing the market. It turned out to be an unexpected success. The market is there and people are buying and selling everyday. We started and grew on eBay, and decided that at some point we really needed to round out our sales channels, so the eBay store was obviously a very natural fit. We built the eBay store but it still isn't open. People are constantly asking us if we're going to open a retail location, but I don't think we ever will.

---

eBay is all about bidders, because the only way the price is going to rise on a product is when you get more than one person bidding.

Your statistics are great; you have a 99.9 % positive feedback rating. Your volumes are incredible. People are obviously satisfied with your products and service.

I would say so. This has been an incredibly low margin business. The consumers are definitely winning. It's not extremely profitable, but we feel we are building up a great base of customers who are thrilled with the product that we sell, as well as the service that we provide.

Are you getting the photographs of your items from the manufacturers? They are very professional looking.

Thank you very much. No. That is totally done in-house. We take all the products in-house and we process them, take pictures of them, and write the descriptions ourselves.

Well, that takes capital on your end, but there are a lot of benefits for you to warehouse the products yourself.

We have a lot of control. Being able to close the loop and have excellent communication with the customer is really important. We let them know exactly what's happening at each step of the process, so they receive the product just as we promised. It really is the cornerstone of why we have a 99.9% positive feedback rating. I believe that there are only fourteen other eBay users worldwide who have a higher ranking than ours.

With that kind of volume and that kind of feedback you have a phenomenal record.

Thank you. We're proud of it.

Does any of your experience from college help you in your business?

Yes. I was a Business Administration major. So I learned the basics.

Do you go to events like eBay Live ?

Not typically. If they have an event for the top sellers, which they do on occasion, we'll attend. In general we're so far ahead of the curve that there's very little that eBay can teach us. There are some technical aspects of eBay's services like new products and features that they roll out that are important for us to know about, but in general they ask us questions about the marketplace and about what's happening on the seller's side. A lot of folks that work at eBay have never worked for large sellers on eBay. They typically don't know what it looks like from our side. They frequently have worked for large technology companies. They could just as easily be working for Siemens or AOL. They don't really have a grasp on what it's like to take in 2,500 pairs of shoes and turn them around, catalog them, and box them. They don't understand the logistical side of things. We're frequently asked to present at those kinds of events, but we typically don't attend. While we want to be part of the community, the last thing we want to do is generate more competition. The people at the top at the eBay headquarters are incredibly keyed in, but the administrative types below them have a hard time relating to what's happening in the field.

Have you ever talked to Meg Whitman or seen her at an eBay event?

Yes. My partner and I have met her.

Are you using any kind of auction management service?

We certainly are. We're using a company called ChannelAdvisor. They are a private company but eBay has invested in them. We've found them to be the best in terms of their services and their connection with eBay.

Do they email for you and keep track of the money coming in?

ChannelAdvisor has auction management software that provides a comprehensive one-stop solution for managing inventory. They handle everything from feedback and emails, to payment notification.

There's another one called AuctionWorks. Are they about the same as AuctionWorks?

I think they'd be in the same category. I can't speak intelligently about AuctionWorks because I know nothing about them.

Did you use ChannelAdvisor from the beginning or did you add them as your business grew?

We've been with ChannelAdvisor for about nine months. Prior to that we ran the business using Excel, believe it or not.

Well, hey. You see quite a difference now.

An incredible difference.

I see some of your items have a Buy-It-Now option, but most of them start out with a minimum bid. Right?

Yes. That is correct.

Why do you put a Buy-It-Now option for some of the items but not others?

We use the Buy-It-Now option for products we're deep in.

Do you also use a Dutch auction for that?

No. We don't participate in Dutch auctions. We provide the Buy-It-Now as a secondary means for people to purchase the products we're deep in.

Would you have a starting bid of a penny on the Buy-It-Now option as well?

No. With the Buy-It-Now option the price is just the same as the Buy-It-Now price.

So it's just a regular sale then?

Yes. There are some people who don't really understand what's happening and place the bid on the opening bid instead of hitting Buy-It-Now, and they wait for the auction to end. There are a couple of nuances that take some knowledge of eBay procedures to understand.

Could you tell me what a Dutch auction is all about?

Sure. A Dutch auction occurs when you're putting up for auction more than one item in a single auction. I'll try and simplify it, because it's complicated. I'll stick with the two-bidder system. If the auction ended with only one person bidding on two items at two dollars and the other person bidding on one item for one dollar, then both bidders would win the items for one dollar. That means the person who was willing to bid two dollars got the two items for a dollar each, because nobody else pushed the bids higher. It's possible that in this scenario somebody says, "I'm willing to pay $100 for one of the items," but if the other bidders are only willing to pay a dollar, then the person who bid $100 will get the item for a dollar.

If somebody else came in and bid three dollars for two of the items and one person still just had the one at one dollar, then it would be over at one dollar. Right?

Yes. But if Bidder "C" comes in and you had one at one dollar, two at two dollars, and then a third bidder bid for two of them at three dollars and the auction ended, the person who bid three dollars would get two of them for two dollars, and the person that bid two dollars would get one of them for two dollars.

The high bidder would get the quantity they wanted and the low bidder would get what was left over.

Exactly.

Do they have to accept one if they bid for two?

No.

A person could say, "I don't want it then, because I wanted two."

Right. Exactly. It is pretty complicated!

So you never use reserves.

We never use reserves. We win some, we lose some, but we win more than we lose.

Again, I looked at your photography and it is excellent. I can see why people aren't going to let something go by if they want it.

Absolutely. It is the purest economy in the world. One of the most unique things about where and when we did this is that a year prior to the business starting it probably would not have worked because the critical mass wasn't there. Prior to 2001 eBay did not have critical mass; there would not have been enough bidders to support what we're doing.

Did you ever use a pay-per-click service for your original website?

Yes. We used a pay-per-click service where we paid for ad placement. For Sprint PCS, at some point I think it went as high as two dollars a click. Pay-per-click is how I drove business to that site.

Were your visitors buying something or just looking?

I got about a 15% conversion rate. I thought it was great at the time. The vast majority was not buying. They were probably just doing research. But a lot of people did buy. I sold about 300-400 mobile phones a month.

It must have been heartbreaking when Sprint changed their policy.

I think it was the only time that I've ever actually cried because of business. I was absolutely devastated because I had worked so hard and the potential was so great at the time. It was one of those situations where it was almost as if you were water-skiing, and you kept on tripping, and you finally get back on the water-ski's and the boat runs out of gas. [Laughs.] It was absolutely crushing at the time.

How many days do you normally set your auctions for?

The vast majority of them are seven-day auctions. There's very little benefit from going from seven to ten days. I don't really have any scientific evidence to say why, but we've anecdotally found that this is the most effective way for us.

It gives people a chance to have time to decide.

Yes. It's enough time to bring in enough bidders to get it to the level where it needs to be. eBay is all about bidders, because the only way the price is going to rise on a product is when you get more than one person bidding. You could have one person who's willing to buy your shoes for $1000, but if somebody else isn't willing to buy them for $1000 it's never going to rise to that price. You must have two people or preferably three or four to compete against each other.

What has changed since you started selling on eBay?

I'd say the number one change with eBay is the excellence with which they have built and run the technical side of their business. I can remember back in the very early days when eBay's search engine would go down and the site would be unusable for a day. They used to have these technical glitches that have now virtually disappeared. The enormity of what is happening in their database twenty-four hours a day, seven days a week, three hundred and sixty-five days of the year is just amazing.

It's almost hard to comprehend, isn't it?

It really is. The CTO (Chief Technical Officer) will tell you that it's like driving an Indy car and having the pit crew change the tires going 220 miles an hour and not crashing. It's that kind of living on the edge. If you could imagine how many people alone are just trying to hack the system. So I would say the number of bidders is number one and then the awe-inspiring job they do with their IT (Information Technology) is number two.

Did eBay own PayPal when you started?

No. [Laughs.] When we started, PayPal was just a tiny fledgling blip on the screen. I'm more of a big picture thinker and don't think about the details of the business as much as my business partner Jon might. Well, there are actually three of us, myself, Jon Kuhlmann and Mark Fitzgerald. Jon takes care of a lot of those details and he has a lot of anecdotes and stories about what the payment systems used to be like. He started with them right at the beginning when they were really, really small.

Did most people pay by check or credit card when you started?

We definitely promoted PayPal right off the bat. The reason they're as large as they are and eBay bought them is because their value brought users quickly to their service. PayPal has always been a cornerstone of our payment method and continues to be so today. It's impossible for me to put a number on it, but more than the majority of people are using PayPal. We have switched over to also allowing people to pay directly with credit cards, so that has been a growing segment. The checks have always been there. We've always accepted them. There are still segments of our customer base that are skittish about actually "buying something online" and they still feel most comfortable sending in a check or money order.

If something's working eBay will invest in it or buy it. What innovative things do you think eBay might come up with in the future?

It sounds cheesy, but I feel like it's hard to improve on perfection. All these new features and services they roll out are conveniences that add more sparkle. In general the core competency of their product is so basic and so pure...the only thing they can do is develop systems to attract additional buyers that are more horizontal in their purchasing. I had a conversation with somebody on a plane a couple months ago and the person had been buying and selling collectibles for years. He had a rating in the thousands and he had never considered buying shoes on eBay. The thought of buying shoes on eBay was just totally foreign to him even though eBay was something that he was using everyday and had become an integral part of his hobby and business. One of the biggest challenges in the future is to get people who are buying and selling collectibles, antiques and automobiles to start thinking about other ways to use eBay. But in terms of innovation, the eBay system works so well that I just can't imagine what they might do in the future. I do, however, think we're in the first 200 yards of a marathon.

For those people interested in starting an eBay business, what would be a good way for them to get their feet wet?

If somebody was really interested I would suggest they go up to their attic or down to their basement and find the most expensive items that they haven't used for the last few years, clean them up, and take some pictures. They should look on eBay to see how other people are presenting, say ski boots or a set of skis that they haven't been using. Take the pictures in the same way the best people are presenting them on eBay and give it a whirl. See what it's about. Many people are bright eyed and excited about launching the business and there's a tremendous amount of people who have access to the right types of products to put on eBay. But selling on eBay is definitely not for everybody; it's not very easy. Typically eBay buyers are an incredibly frugal bunch, who demands a lot for nothing. So if you're going to sell on eBay you have to be ready to make very little money while providing ultimate customer service. People get angry and upset if we send out an automatic response to a question and will send us a three paragraph letter about "where do I send my check?" [Laughs.] You would also not believe the excuses I get for why somebody can't complete a transaction for buying a pair of shoes. I would say if you're looking to start a business, the best thing to do is look around and sell some things. One of the most interesting things about eBay is how it creates a value on almost every single thing you own. Never before was there any value, short of a garage sale, in your salt shakers. eBay provides a value. This is why the shoe business works. Anything with a brand name associated with it has value. So people can start out by selling shirts that they haven't worn in two years. Maybe they've got a couple Polo shirts and the colors are out of fashion now. If they've got some sorbet light color shirts; selling those might be a good way for somebody to get their feet wet.

Where did you come up with your website name grapevinehill.com and your eBay User ID "grapevinehill"?

As part of my marketing background I realized we needed to have a marketable name, something that our customers and vendors wouldn't devalue. We didn't want to name ourselves something like The Shoe Shack or Cheap Shoes Online or Shoe Discount Warehouse. We decided we were going to have a formal brand name. My business partners and I met at Gordon Collage, which is in Wenham, Massachusetts. We were going to name it Grapevine Road, but grapevineroad.com was taken by a folk band in Maine. I was on the phone with one of my partners, Jon, discussing what we were going to do. We were thinking of Big Red Barn, or something of that nature. I noticed my wife had received a Garnet Hill catalog and a light bulb went off and I said, "How about Grapevinehill?" So that's how it happened.

So you had kept in touch with your fellow students from college. Had you ever done business with them before starting Grapevinehill?

Yes. I kept in touch with one of my fellow students in particular, Jon. He was just out of college and I had gotten kicked out of college back in 1992 or 1993. Together we started Fat Bottom Titanium, which was a bike component company. It was only in business for about two years. Our supply got cut off because the defense factory that was producing our goods was shut down. We were making bar ends, handlebars, seat posts and the stem part that attaches the handlebar. Then we were also in another business together called Guerrilla Billboards, which was a mobile billboard company. We had all kept in contact and we were good friends so it was natural. Each one of us has a different skill set. I think we have a powerful team.

Mike Wuertz

Keeps Up On Trends

He knows when to change course. Mike Wuertz has the ability to look at a market and determine what position in the demand curve a product is in. He instinctively knows when to focus on specific products. By analyzing the market he is able to satisfy customer demand and reap success.

Mike, you have a very complete set of games and equipment listed on eBay and your website. Walk us through your available product lines, if you will.

Well, we carry what we call the "vintage games." We've got probably 20,000 Sega Saturn titles in stock, which I'm sure is the most available from anybody in the country. Many years ago we bought out all the inventory of a game distributor in Dallas. That's how we came across those games. Even though Sega Saturn hasn't been made since 1995 or 1996, we still sell hundreds of Sega Saturn titles every week. We have over a hundred titles. We also have 3D0, which hasn't been manufactured since the early to mid 1990's. We carry heavy inventories in the 3D0 product. We're probably one of the largest 3D0 distributors around. We also have some Sega CD products available for sale. The Super Nintendo, believe it or not, is still a very strong market force.

The problem I have there is finding enough products to be able to sell, but they sell extremely well. So a lot of the vintage games do extremely well for us.

They're not making those games anymore?

They're not making those anymore, at all. Next we handle the Playstation 1, Playstation 2, Xbox, Game Cube, GameBoy Advance; all the latest platforms that are out there. We also specialize in what we call "budget" games or "closeout" games. When it first comes out it's a new release game, and at the current time we're not into the new releases. Most of the sites, like eBay and Amazon, charge you fifteen percent to sell the game. There's hardly any profit in a game when it's a new release. As a result, we wait until a few months after it's released for the price to drop down to another tier. Then about six months after it's released it goes to what they call a "budget" title. So a title that originally cost us forty dollars is now down in the fifteen or sixteen dollar range. Generally we pick up our games in that price range.

If you have unique product then I think it's [eBay] an excellent place.

Are you just selling new games?

All we sell is brand new games in the newer format.

I see that some retailers are offering exchange programs.

Hollywood Video and Blockbuster Video have both gone very heavily into exchange programs for games. Electronic Boutique and GameStop, which are probably the two biggest resale game only chains, really make their money through the game exchange.

Do they try to sell the games that they're exchanging?

They sell them. There's a lot more money in a used game than there is in a new game. Hollywood Video, Blockbuster Video, Electronic Boutique and GameStop want to be in that business, because used video games are profitable. The problem with used video games is that the majority of them are sitting in households. How do you acquire the used games? Sometimes you can buy them from video stores, but with the video stores basically dominating eighty percent of the rental business, you've got to get it from the home user. Since these are stores in the local markets, it's much easier for people to take it to the local store and do the exchange as opposed to over the Internet. That's why we don't get into it.

You've been on eBay for quite some time now.

We've been there since 1998. Yes.

You were one of the pioneers!

Actually we were out there prior to 1998 under another name. We changed our eBay User ID to "megabuys.com". We were one of the very first on eBay.

And were you in this field prior to when you started to sell on eBay?

No. I had a video distribution business. We provided a turnkey operation to the Blockbuster video franchise. We would set up their inventory. We competed with Blockbuster Corporate to set up a Blockbuster Video store. We sold various types of products to over 600 Blockbuster stores. We had a lot of hundred thousand dollar plus orders with that company, and we had around eighty employees who put the packages together. The problem we ran into is that as Blockbuster grew, they bought out their franchisees. When they would buy out the franchise, they were buying out our customer base. Originally it was eighty percent franchise and twenty percent corporate stores; then it reversed to about eighty-five percent corporate stores and fifteen percent franchise stores. It just wasn't profitable for us to stay in that business. We tried to sell the business but ended up liquidating. They could save fifteen or twenty thousand dollars per store by buying from us. We sold in Hawaii, Guam, Alaska. We put Blockbuster Video stores in all 50 states.

There were games at that time?

There were games but they weren't as popular as they are today. We were dealing with Nintendo, which were the old eight-bit Nintendo, the Super Nintendo, Playstation 1 and sometimes Sega Saturn. It wasn't quite as big a market as it is today. They did put several hundred games in each video store, and we did the video game packages that they put in their stores. We got into eBay after we held two auctions when we liquidated the business. Some of the people that bid on the items never picked them up at the end of the auction. So I put them on eBay and I couldn't believe how much money I made. I made a trip out to Dallas and there was a video game distributor that had gone bankrupt. We went to the auction and bought six truckloads of video games and we were back in the video game business.

So you auctioned your inventory traditionally and had some left over.

That's correct.

Were you computer literate at that time?

I was one of the first ten or twelve salespeople for NCR in computer sales when I got out of college back in the sixties. So I worked for NCR in computer sales and started my own computer company called National Data. I built that up and sold it way too early. I sold it when we were doing about 28 million a year. After I sold, the company went up to about 500 million a year and then it was sold out to a larger company. I've also owned large chains of video stores; I'd sold out to Movie Gallery in 1996, right after they had gone public. That's about the time Blockbuster was buying out all of their franchise stores, so we decided to liquidate. I was going to retire, but never got there.

Did you list those items on eBay and think, "Geez, people are actually buying these things?"

Yes. It was unbelievable how much they bought and the prices they were paying. Especially for some of the used games that we had back then. Like anything else, eBay has evolved and the video game business is extremely competitive. From a profit structure standpoint it's a pretty tough business; we do have a high overhead. We've got a 7,500 square foot warehouse here and a staff. We have to compete with a Ma and Pa that's working out of their home and doesn't have the overhead or health insurance and everything else.

How many employees do you have?

We're maintaining around ten full-time employees. We have some part-time people and at Christmas we'll go up as high as thirty employees. Around the holidays we'll get as many as 1000 orders a day.

What changes have you seen on eBay since you started?

The competition is the biggest thing. There are over fifty million people on eBay today. A lot of them go into the video game business because they can buy them brand new. If people are satisfied making a few hundred dollars a week, they'll price the games extremely low on eBay. It's a tough business from a profitability standpoint to be on eBay and try to run a large company. It's easier to have a large company that's got excess product and sell it on eBay than it is to try and develop a business around eBay. Then eBay purchased PayPal, which is probably how ninety percent of the people pay over the Internet. They've got their bases pretty well covered. Whether the item sells or not, you still owe that fee to eBay. Some items out there can have 100 listings and only five of them that are going to sell in a week. They're collecting money from 100 different listings, even though only five of them are selling. eBay didn't own PayPal when we started.

How did most people pay?

Most people paid with a credit card or personal check. We were probably selling for around two years before we even signed up for PayPal, but as PayPal developed it really reversed. Originally we had 100 percent of the people paying us by check or by credit card; today 90 percent will pay by PayPal.

As I recall, you're using the gallery photo so customers can see the product.

Yes. We actually just switched software. We had written all of our software until our company got so large that our software couldn't keep up with the number of in-coming orders. When we hit a thousand orders a day it exposed every little problem we had with our software. We made the decision to can our software, in which we had invested almost $200,000. We chose a company out of North Carolina called ChannelAdvisor because their software satisfied our needs. We've been in the midst of a conversion for probably two months over to that software. Hopefully within the next 2 weeks all the products will be converted to ChannelAdvisor's software. We have to get some additional software for inventory systems.

You generally charge one price. Is that the Buy-It-Now option?

Yes. Originally we had the auction format, but we found that over eighty percent of people were using the Buy-It-Now option. So we decided to simplify the format and use the Buy-It-Now option.

Have they added any options since you started?

Well, originally eBay didn't have the Buy-It-Now feature. It was strictly a bid process. Of course, they charge the person a nickel just to use that Buy-It-Now feature. They can charge you a quarter to use the gallery feature. If you have a reserve there's a reserve fee. If you want to put it in your eBay store, there's a separate fee for that too. If you ever analyze the fee structure on one of my auctions, it's really pretty high. You make a lot of money on the freight, as opposed to on the item itself.

Did you buy the new software that you're using now?

We bought the software and we pay them a percentage of our sales.

Is it similar to AuctionWorks?

It's similar to AuctionWorks. That is correct.

Did you have your own software prior to that?

Yes. eBay kept coming out with so many changes to their software I was either going to have to hire a couple of programmers just to keep up, or go with somebody else. We couldn't keep up with the amount of changes to the software, so that's why we made the decision to change.

On your website, how much of the business comes directly to you and bypasses eBay?

Not much, less than ten percent of the business comes directly to our site. We used to be on Amazon too, but as we are switching software we decided to hold back on Amazon until we feel our software on eBay is running sufficiently.

Did you feel like you almost had to license your own software, if you were going to spend the money to keep up with eBay?

Well, that's true. ChannelAdvisor has a team of programmers who work with eBay. They have a large staff. I had one or two people who were trying to do what they have twenty people doing. It was impossible to keep up with all the changes that they had.

Are you using anything like a pay-per-click advertising service on your site?

No. We are not. We have looked into that. We're going to be expanding quite a bit in the DVD area. We're currently running a few hundred items on eBay and it's very successful for us.

Are they going to be newer releases?

Most of them will be older releases. We've gone heavily into the eBay stores and we're going to the gallery feature on the eBay stores. If you analyze by using your software and realize an item doesn't sell frequently enough, you can put it on eBay stores. For example, let's take an item at $9.95 and an item at $14.95. If it's under $9.95 and you list it on eBay, it costs about thirty-five cents. If the item you list is $10.00 to $24.95, it's going to cost you seventy cents. Then you have the gallery fee of a nickel. You can put it in your eBay store and it only costs you 3 cents a month. If you can lead people to your eBay store, then you don't have all those listing fees. If an item doesn't sell, you can't afford to leave it on eBay. By putting it in the eBay store, it saves us a lot in the listing fees. The other advantage is we couldn't sell the new items, because the eBay fees are too much in relation to the amount of profit. If a brand new Xbox or Playstation 2 game comes out today, our cost would be somewhere around forty dollars. If you go to Hollywood Video, Target or Wal-Mart, you can buy the game for around forty-eight dollars. There's only a twenty percent margin. If your item closes, you're paying five percent on the first twenty-five dollars and two percent on anything over twenty-five dollars. Then you're paying PayPal a thirty-cent transaction fee plus two percent of whatever the people pay through PayPal. When you start adding all these fees, you've got three dollars worth of fees to PayPal and to eBay just to sell an item that someone can go to Wal-Mart and buy for the same price. Since it's only costing us three cents at the eBay store, if we can guide people to the store then we can save on all those listing fees. Then it does become practical to put an item out there.

I think everybody wants to be in business for herself or himself; eBay certainly provides that channel.

Then they see that when they click on the description?

Actually we haven't really done that yet, but we plan on doing that.

That could be interesting.

That would be a whole new area for us.

It could be huge.

Okay, now don't hold me to this figure exactly. If I remember correctly, in eBay's game category they made 140 million in sales. That's just on eBay. It's a huge business out there. eBay's figure is growing constantly as far as the amount of games, and it's even heavier on DVD and book.

Do you see evolution in the game industry?

Well, one of the big things that is happening is being able to download games over the Internet. If somebody wants a game they can just go to a website and download a game right to their machine as opposed to having to go and buy it from a store. I believe you can also go online and play. If you're in California and want to play with somebody here in Florida, you can go online. You can even compete against each other over the Internet.

Do you see any way you can fit into that?

We haven't really looked into that. We have our niche. We're not looking to be all encompassing.

Specifically what suggestions would you give to someone who wants to start an eBay business?

It's hard to start a business selling on eBay, because it is so competitive out there. A lot of the people selling are not businesspeople, and have no idea what their total cost is to sell an item on eBay. You have to figure your listing, your closing, and all your PayPal fees. Some people just want to make a little bit of additional money and from a profitability standpoint if they make $1.00 or $2.00 they're perfectly happy. Building a business beyond that is extremely tough to do.

You've got fifty million competitors out there in a way.

A lot of whom are not good businesspeople and do not analyze costs. They aren't going to be around for a long time, but they are going to be there long enough to mess you up on pricing. If you have a unique product then I think it's an excellent place. I was at a recent meeting and met a fellow who imported a building product from China. He was doing 100,000 a month on eBay with a sixty-five percent gross profit margin. It was a home building product. He had found a niche and he was making a ton of money. We have to deal in volume. If we can do 500 orders a day and make money then we can come out okay. We've got to create a large number of orders due to how cheap we sell the product. It's a volume deal for us.

Are most of your sales in the United States or overseas?

We do a lot of business overseas. I believe we've sold to around 137 different countries. Canada's huge. It's basically like the United States. We also sell a tremendous amount in England and Australia. Germany is an extremely good market for eBay. We sell to the Latin American countries, Africa, China and Russia. It's worldwide with the Internet.

Is eBay concentrating on the Japanese market?

I am not sure. A fellow I dealt with at Amazon was in charge of setting up Amazon in Japan and I think they do pretty well over there. Japan is not one of the countries we do a lot of business with. From my understanding, Japan doesn't have free Internet as we have free Internet over here. It costs you so much for the amount of time you're on the Internet there, and as a result the Internet has not spread as rapidly in Japan as it has in some of the other countries.

Do you sell equipment to play the games as well?

No. Only if we pick them up on a deal. Every once in a while somebody will have 100 to 150 machines at special price and we'll pick them up and sell them. On a normal basis, the amount of profit is less than ten percent. To try and take that and put it on eBay is not practical.

Are the machines usually new when you find them?

Generally they're new machines. We do sell some used machines and we still have some Sega Saturn and 3D0 machines. We had several hundred Super Nintendo machines but we sold them. We used to do a lot of business with accessories, but the problem is that we ship using the U.S. Postal Office. We used to ship by media mail, but you cannot ship an accessory item by media mail. The freight has become so high on the accessories that we've really backed down quite a bit due to the charge. It's such a large portion of the overall cost.

So you can't send an accessory through mail?

Well, you can send it through the mail. But you can't send it by media mail and media mail is cheaper. You can ship a CD or a Playstation 1 game by media mail, but you cannot ship an accessory item by media mail.

Are there some things you would like to add which might be important or interesting?

I would add that it's important to look at the fee structure. You basically have brackets as to where the item sells. For us it's under $9.95, $10.00 to $24.95, and $25 and over. You have a listing fee based on what you're listing. On top of that, if you want to put the item in a gallery you have to pay a nickel fee. Whether the item sells or not, you're paying that listing fee. If you have an item at $14.95 and you have it listed for three days, it costs you seventy cents whether the item sells or does not sell. You can list it a second time and if it does sell the second time, then you only have to pay one listing fee, not two. It's got to sell the very next time, though, and you need to have software to be able to do that. You have your listing fee to start out with. Then you have a closing fee. The closing fee is based upon a percentage of the price of the item for which it sells. If it's under $25 then eBay's going to take five percent as their closing fee. Ninety percent of eBay customers are going to pay for that item by PayPal. PayPal has a thirty cent transaction fee, and will charge anywhere from 1.9 to 2.9 percent of the sale price based upon how much business you do with PayPal in a given month. Then depending on the software you use you have a lot of different fees. We pay a percentage of our sales to the software company. If you're selling a $14.95 item, it could cost you $2.50 just in fees to sell that item. You've got fees even if the item does not sell.

It's important for people starting a business to go in with their eyes open and be aware of their costs. Costs can certainly add up.

I had a 3 month period from December to February where I paid eBay $67,000 in fees. That doesn't include PayPal, or software companies or anything! The fee structure costs a lot and you better know what you're doing or you're not going to make any money. It depends on how big a seller you want to be; we are one of the larger sellers on eBay. There's a guy in California who sells over a quarter million a month on eBay. He sells from 20,000 to 30,000 DVD's a month on eBay.

Well maybe you can get into his market. (Laughs)

Well, we are looking at his market because we're very familiar with it and we're set up with all the same suppliers. He says that video games are one of the markets that he wants to get into. We're doing extremely well and we will be expanding in that market. The basic thing is the fee structure and also the product that you're going to sell. I've met a lot of people who sell clothing, I've met people who sell swimming pool supplies, and I've met people who sell construction products. There's a person who was primarily on Half.com, owned by eBay, and Amazon.com, and he was doing $150,000 a month just selling books.

Is there any advantage from a profit margin standpoint of using eBay over Amazon?

One of the advantages of eBay is you can set your own freight policies. On Amazon, you can't do that. Amazon's the one that makes all the money on freight, not the sellers.

If you have an item on eBay for $14.95, people are thinking, well, that's $14.95! But if there's a five-dollar shipping charge, there should be a little margin in there.

Then you have your Targets and your Kmarts and your Hollywoods and your Blockbusters that basically sell video games. They want to sell whatever they make the most money on per square foot, because they've got a limited amount of square feet available in each store. So they're selling the latest hot items out there and they can't afford to carry and display an item that is only going to sell once a month. That's where the Internet comes in. We can sell an item that will only sell once a month in the store. If you take five thousand stores across the country, then that's where we get our volume. It's nothing like the new release or anything else, but it's an item that stores can't afford to stock. The natural place to find that item is on the Internet.

In your wildest dreams, when you were with NCR did you visualize what was going to happen?

Yes, I thought I had the computer industry pegged, but my visions really burned out in the late 1980's to the early 1990's. It's going far beyond wherever I thought it would go.

Can you see where the Internet is going in the future?

There will be so many services offered online. I think movies, games and music will all be downloaded at home. I just don't think the retailer is going to be the mass merchant he is today. I'm sure something will come along and replace him. So much of it will be downloaded directly to the household, or to some unit like an MP3 player. We'll be dinosaurs someday.

Do you have anything else to add?

I think everybody wants to be in business for herself or himself; eBay certainly provides that channel. Whether they will make money at it is another question.

Brandon Dupsky

Working a Plan

Starting from scratch. Brandon Dupsky started his business in a coffee shop with a well thought out plan. He has the ability to look at the big picture and put it together piece by piece as if it were a jigsaw puzzle. His flexibility allows him to alter his course when necessary by digesting gathered, pertinent facts and opinions before making a decision.

So Brandon, how long have you been on eBay?

Well, around six years now.

You process overstocks and returns on eBay, then help people turn them back into cash. Correct?

Yes. Our focus is on surplus inventory. We help companies liquidate their surplus inventory over the Internet. It has become kind of a hot topic. Six years ago it was a new concept.

You offer a much needed service for people looking to move overstocked inventory; your use of warehouse space and ability to sell overstocked goods is a great business concept. What kind of background did you have before getting involved with Internet services like eBay?

My background comes from supply chain management, and an operations and logistics environment, rather than a technical environment. My experience was largely with warehousing, inventory management and forecasting.

Did this business exist before you started out on eBay? Or did you start this company yourself?

Sell2All was actually a company that I started myself.

Did you have your own business before? Or were you working for someone else up to that point?

I started doing this as a hobby, when I was working a regular 9 to 5 job for a large corporation. In the evenings and on weekends I worked on the concept of selling surplus inventory through eBay. I felt as though I were living two lives for awhile.

It sounds like you have a lot of natural entrepreneurial abilities! So Brandon, tell me more about the growth of your company. I heard that you have been in five different buildings in Lincoln, Nebraska. Is that correct?

We've moved three times. Our current location is actually our fourth.

That is a lot of moving around in only six years. I understand that you're warehousing some items. Do some of your clients keep the products until you've sold them and then deal with shipping?

There are two or three basic scenarios. In one scenario, we'll function as a traditional liquidator. Someone will shoot us their inventory and we will buy it from them. We'll take it off their hands and pay cash for the inventory. We buy items and then resell them for ourselves. In another scenario, we'll bring in inventory on consignment. Through consignment a company lets items sit here, and then we sell the items and ship them on the company's behalf. Consignment is not a large piece of our business. Yet another scenario is drop shipping. Through drop shipping we sell a company's items and they ship the items directly to our customers.

With drop shipping do your customers keep items until they're sold or do you warehouse most of the items?

We warehouse most of the items.

So you need a lot of space.

Yes. We need a lot of space. I would say we buy and resell 60 percent, we drop ship 30 percent, and we consign around 10 percent.

Browsing through your online space, it looks like most of the items come with a Buy-It-Now option. The Buy-It-Now option allows an eBay bidder to automatically win the auction by paying a set price. There's one price, and that is what the item sells for. Is that basically how your company is set up?

On eBay, yes. A lot of items now have a Buy-It-Now option because we want to turn the inventory quickly. We might get a palette of 200 or 300 DVD players, and if we put them up for auction it would take too long to sell them. By the time we sold the last DVD player our company would be losing money, because DVD players depreciate in price quickly.

I noticed that a photograph accompanies most of your items, giving the customer an opportunity to see the item before they click on the link. You have a whole variety of merchandise, everything from camcorders, tools and audio equipment. I think I even saw a game on there somewhere.

I'm not sure about the game. We do sell a wide variety of products because almost every industry has a surplus inventory. Fortunately our services can be spread across multiple product categories.

You have a program where you actually sell individual items for other people?

Yes, DropPro. We recently started that.

So you're going to align yourself with other retailers and do the selling for them?

Well, it's an interesting concept, because I was actually getting my MBA before I started this business. I wrote a business plan for a company in an entrepreneur class. The model for the business plan involved opening up retail stores all across the country where people could bring their items in to be sold on eBay. It was a concept that I had back in 1998. I went to business plan competitions for the university and other venture capital groups, and the judges kept saying, "You would go out of business with this high cost, retail environment over structure." In multiple cities and in multiple competitions, the judges all identified that as a flaw in the plan. They said, "Open up warehouses and become more centralized. Focus on the business side of it." So that's what I've been doing for the first five or six years of this business. The drop-off concept started gaining attention last year. There are actually a lot of companies out there now doing just that. So, I dusted off my business plan and reviewed it. I tried to figure out what we could do differently and still have a good business model. We ended up deciding to re-launch a brand new business called DropPro. We built the software and the technology to support it, which was a project in itself; it took us about six to eight months. Now we are partnering up with packaging stores, antique stores and retailers to help them offer DropPro services in their community.

Then they take the photograph and keep the item?

It can go many ways. It depends on whom you're talking to. Of course, packaging stores like to pack and ship and they usually have some space in their back office. Most packaging stores would be interested in taking a picture of the item and creating a description, which is what we call "merchandising the item." Once the item sells, they ship it to the customer.

So they warehouse items until they're sold, then you collect the money and send them their piece? That is a great concept because you don't need to have all of your own retail outlets with that overhead.

Yeah, it is a good business model. It will be interesting to see how it unfolds because it's still very new.

Do you have just the one location now?

We have two beta [test] locations and we have a third one opening in a couple weeks. We have about six to eight people who are interested. We also have large retailers who might roll this out nationwide. It's up in the air right now as to how fast this thing will grow, but we see it picking up momentum later in the year.

There is also software for managing people's businesses when they have multiple eBay listings. Have you designed your own software for that?

Oh, yes. We've built all of our technology in-house. I have a whole team of programmers working for me here.

Can you tell me about Auction Remote?

It's a new tool that we launched and made available to all eBay sellers, when we were at eBay Live this year. We designed Auction Remote for our own purposes in 2000. We were growing quickly and had people complaining that they couldn't find their items in all the listings, because it was hard to group the items and search for them. We came up with the concept of a remote control for people to be able to click on a button. You program the buttons on the remote control to find the items for which you want it to search. This was before eBay Stores existed and one of the benefits was to help categorize our items. After eBay Stores came out we realized that while the stores were good for grouping or sub grouping items, they were not good at promoting them. So Auction Remote was a pre eBay Store solution for us. Auction Remote offered us the benefit of promoting our items on holidays, like Mother's Day, Father's Day and Valentines Day. It's a promotional tool which uses advanced search technology for a group of items or a group of holiday type items. Because it is centralized, it provides a lot of convenience.

Is Auction Remote used like a remote control for a television set?

It's like a TV remote, but it's not actually a physical remote. It's just an image of a remote control on your computer screen. We incorporate the existing concept of a remote control that people are familiar with and program it to search auctions.

Does the remote point to all eBay sellers' items or only the items that your subscriber has listed?

It is programmed for the subscriber's specific store front listings. They have the freedom to program the buttons to do whatever they want. It is a promotional tool with one remote per seller.

How does someone find this remote?

If you go to the auctionremote.com website, there is a "How It Works" section that provides a sample of the remote and how it works. It is programmed right into their auction, so when a customer clicks on any one of their items, a picture says "open up my remote control."

I notice that you offer several levels of features.

Yes. Right now we have two levels, Silver and Gold. We are working on building the Platinum and Titanium levels. They will have additional features which will be beneficial for larger sellers, as they go from Silver to Titanium.

You are really on the cutting edge.

Sometimes we feel we are on the edge.

You really have quite an internal system. The company that you recently purchased, Rhea Solutions...

Yes. Rhea Solutions was a web hosting company. We acquired their company earlier this year to repurpose their technology, infrastructure, programs and services. We have since rolled that into what we call "Sell2All Web Services," in order to offer website and web management type services to other people.

Would you be doing graphics and setting that up for them as well as hosting their eBay site?

We're still in the development stage of redesigning what it will do, but we are already hosting some customers' websites - although, not on eBay in this case. We also manage people's storefronts on eBay. It falls under that same umbrella of services. We also have some new tools that we will be launching very soon which will also fall under "Sell2All Web Services." We've taken this other company and put it into our fold of operations. Now we're really going out there and trying to figure out the strategic plans of that department.

So you can use the same software that you're using to manage your program for someone else?

Yes. We manage other people's storefronts on eBay sometimes. Usually large accounts; we don't do it for small accounts. With our company managing their system, they get the advantage of using the technology that we built.

What is Bidmix.com?

Bidmix.com is an import-export marketplace. It's another company we purchased almost two years ago now. Bidmix. com is focused on importing and exporting and it has an international flavor. There are a lot of companies worldwide who will register their company and then register their products. They post ads or products for sale, or things that they want to buy. Bidmix.com has received global exposure, and it actually has a lot of activity in Asia.

Do you have Bidmix.com in other languages, or is it all in English?

It's all in English at this point, which is prohibiting some of the world users from using the software. Still, there are a lot of language translation programs out there that can convert English into their home language.

Bidmix.com sounds like it could help companies expose their products to the international market ...

It's a little ahead of its time right now. International trade happens, but it's still more traditional. That's where you have relationships, customs and brokers. This marketplace is probably going to flourish in the years to come, when global trade becomes a lot easier to manage on a hands free basis.

If you had to go out there and duplicate what you have, it would be extremely expensive.

We have a lot of things that would be hard to copy. The technology, the people, the experience and the business process design - in addition to some of the marketplaces, brand names and reputations associated with our company. Relationships are definitely very valuable.

...you should focus on things that you enjoy, whether it's a product group, a type of service, or a type of item.

How many people did you start out with, other than yourself?

Just myself in the beginning. Then I hired three interns. That was before we really had an office. I was still working out of my house. We used to have meetings at restaurants or at the university, places like that. We just had to wing it to begin with, but we found ourselves an office about three months after I hired everyone.

So you had three interns, and you met in coffee shops and such ... Are they still with you now?

The first intern I hired still works here.

So you picked a pretty good one!

Yes. I have a lot of people who have worked here for around three or four years. My management team, if you add it up, has about 22 years of experience working with me in a six-year-old company.

That business plan and the exposure it received must have been a very beneficial experience. In graduate school did you learn the skills to write a business plan?

I was getting my MBA, and at the same time, I had a hobby that I was trying to turn into a business. So, going to class and learning about subjects and case studies was very valuable. What you learn is up to you to a certain degree, and in this case I had something right in front of me to which I could apply my knowledge. Because I had a business in hand, a real live business, the return I got from my education was probably much better than that of the average person. I could relate the topics to something real right away, making it easier to remember, apply and use the concepts we covered.

Were you working at the time you went for your MBA?

Yes. I was also working full-time.

That's incredible. What was your major as an undergraduate?

It was a business degree. I took a few years off and went out into the corporate world before going back and getting my MBA part time. So, I got a business degree and then an MBA.

Even before you went to college, did you think you might want to get into a business?

I used to think I was going to be an architect.

Well, you are an architect! [Laughs.]

Yes, but in the early days when I was at school for architecture, I was managing in the restaurant business. It was probably around 15 years ago now. I helped build restaurant chains while still going to school, and I realized that I liked building businesses better than building buildings. I caught on to this realization a couple years after architectural college.

Do you ever plan to go public?

Who knows?

Do you have options for your employees? Do they have any equity or incentives in that way?

Yes. All the employees have a stake in the business. That's part of their reward for commitment.

And you're not leaving it out of the picture that you might go public someday?

Who knows? Whatever makes sense at the time.

Where do you see this going? If you had a crystal ball, where would you see it going in the next, you know, five or ten years? Or is that too hard?

Oh, jeez... five years is a long time in the Internet. This thing has momentum. We have an infrastructure that's finally starting to hold solid. We have a lot of good things going for us, and it's starting to allow us to grow upwards faster. We've built this thing to scale. We might be following paths similar to other companies, who are just ahead of us by a few years, like Overstock.com, or like uBid.com. It could be like eBay was five years ago. I see us growing rapidly, continuing to morph. Things are going change a little bit, but I see us as almost like a large Wal-Mart. I see us running as an Internet discount retailer someday. That's it in a nutshell. We provide similar value to the buying customer. Right now, our selection is a lot more limited than theirs, but our competitive price structure is not. We're able to go out there and offer brand new merchandise to the public for better prices than they would find at Best Buy, Circuit City or Wal-Mart. We're going to keep building relationships, and we're going to continue to diversify into new product categories, and we're going to continue to widen the selection and increase the depth of our products.

Some of the people you are buying the overstocks and returns from might want to take the next step and do it themselves through your systems. Will that hurt business?

Most of the people that we help are not manufacturers or distributors. They're usually retailers already, and they're actually in competition with us. We've partnered with them because of our specialization in this process. I would like to believe that we can sell on eBay more professionally, efficiently, intelligently and profitably than anybody else. I've built this business model to be very good at selling products on eBay. These other companies, they use our service because they can't do it themselves as cheaply, or as efficiently. We've positioned ourselves to be tough competitors on a one-on-one level. We've got a lot of things in our favor in relation to cost structure. One of them is as simple as location. I'm located in Lincoln, Nebraska, which is a very low-cost environment to run part of my operations. I get a highly educated workforce at a low cost compared to owning a business in somewhere like California. So, I've got an operational infrastructure that's efficient and cost effective. That's going to be hard to duplicate, which is certainly a competitive advantage for us.

Most people don't have anywhere near the vision that you have. What advice would you give to someone who is trying to start his or her own Internet business?

It's really a lot of fun. But you have to look at it as a business, where you have revenues and you have costs, and every decision you make impacts a plus or a minus in all those things. To allow a business to be successful you should focus on things that you enjoy, whether it's a product group, a type of service, or a type of item. For example, if you like coins, you should focus on coins. If you like fishing, then focus on fishing equipment - something that you enjoy, of course. Focus on doing that well before you start to spread yourself thin. If eBay says there are 430,000 people making a living on eBay, it's possible. It's very possible.

And you're one of the top ten sellers on eBay now, out of around 430,000.

Out of 55 million, but 430,000 who make a living out of it.

191

[Laughs.] Okay. 55 million? That's incredible! And I'm sure however many are left would like to be making a living, right?

Well, they sell something here and there, or they buy something here and there.

I'm very interested in seeing DropPro. That's an interesting concept.

There are a lot of people doing it, so it's going to be a very competitive environment in the next couple of years. It is going to grow like crazy.

I know eBay has seller assistance to help people sell their items. If most people only have a few items, I don't think they would go through the procedure of learning how to load them on eBay. It's probably better to take them to DropPro and have you do it.

eBay predicts it will be a 20 billion dollar industry. I'm not certain it's going to be that big, but of course I think it's a huge market opportunity. We'll see, I guess.

Are you going to eBay Live this year? Have you been going regularly to their events?

We go annually, and I'm taking seven people this year.

What do they usually do there at their events?

There are usually 10,000 people there. It's going to be the average people who sell on eBay and make a living doing so, and it's probably going to be out of the upper half of those 430,000 people. They have booths with services and software to help support your eBay business, and then they have breakout sessions. There are training sessions on key topics, such as how to hire good employees, how to market your items, and how to merchandise your store. It's a very fun event and I enjoy going every year.

Have you had any opportunity to talk with the chairman [Meg Whitman] there?

Meg? I have met her about three or four times now, but have only spoken to her briefly.

I've seen her just on TV. She's very impressive.

Absolutely! She's a billion dollar woman. She's done some impressive things.

Pretty incredible. … So when you have thousands of items you have to manage them all internally. Correct?

Yes. I started in the early days when there really weren't too many software companies out there. There were a few of them and they kept approaching me, saying, "Hey, use our software. Use our software." My opinion back then was, "I don't know if you're going to be in business tomorrow. And so if you go out of business, then I can't sell on eBay anymore. It hurts my business." So I built my own software for the sake of control. I wanted to make sure that no one's business could impact mine. A lot of software companies back then did go out of business, so I'm happy I didn't decide to choose one, because I could have easily chosen the wrong one. Back then we were building our own software at the same time those other companies were, but we built it for our own needs versus a general need, so it's more focused.

Exactly. You have the flexibility to do exactly what you need to do for your needs rather than trying to tweak things at your end to work through somebody else's system. I've heard of an auction management service called AuctionWorks. Are they the biggest auction management service?

Yes. AuctionWorks is probably the biggest. They have been in business for quite a while and they have one of the best reputations, of course.

Who are some of the other prominent businesses?

The two biggest ones are probably ChannelAdvisor and AuctionWorks. I don't know if you've heard of ChannelAdvisor. They're out of North Carolina. There are actually a lot of auction management service companies. Then you have Andale and Auctiva.

What kind of hours do you keep? Is it a seven day a week job for you?

It almost is. I have to log in everyday from home, and I log in at night from home. I have two kids, so playing with them is my first priority when I get home, of course. But after they're asleep, it's a matter of catching up and working on small projects here and there. It is a full time job and a half; it's been a sixty, seventy hour a week job for the last six years.

Do you have any specific physical exercise routines that you follow?

I love to work. I've basically eliminated everything else right now. Work and family are the two things for me.

Well those are good priorities. The kids will keep you balanced, right?

Oh yeah. They're at a fun age right now.

You have a unique situation with your internal software and the size of your business. You've done very, very well with the original business plan you wrote. Most people don't do anything like that. I noticed on your website that you are partners with Hollywood Direct. What is your relationship with them? What is your relationship with other partners?

Partnerships ... Some of them are just people that we do business with. We manage some of their software or storefronts. I don't know if I'd call them partnerships, but I have a lot of friendships with other eBay sellers. Outside of just running a business, it's valuable to build relationships with other sellers from regularly attending seller summits and conferences. This enables you to build strong networks with other people who are trying to do very similar things. I put value on that, because I can call up a friend across the country that has his own little business. He might be doing something similar or better than me, and we can help each other out. I may ask, "How did you solve this, or how did you do that?" I wouldn't really call those partnerships, but I would call those tight relationships. Those are things that I've nurtured over the years. I gave you some of my advice for people selling on eBay: pick a focus, find something you like, and run it like a business. You've got to constantly change;

in this environment the competition is at your heels. We go out and launch something. Then somebody else will find the same item and try to sell it for a dollar cheaper. They'll copy the description and marketing approach. We have focused on trying to be a moving target, which takes a lot of energy. You need to position yourself so that you can't be copied and put out of business.

Ingredients for Success

I promised at the beginning of the book to recap some of the valuable messages that stand out to me. I am sure you will find other messages as well that will be of great significance to you. Here are the recurrent themes that impressed me most from listening to these successful entrepreneurs' stories.

Have a Strong Work Ethic

Bill Cameta

> *The number one thing is you have to be willing to work and think, to work and think, work and think, and work and think.*

Brandon Dupsky

> *I love to work. I've basically eliminated everything else right now. Work and family are the two things to me. It's a full time job and a half; it's been a sixty, seventy hour a week job for the last six years.*

Chuck Black

Of course I work a lot more hours now than I ever did before, but it's much more rewarding.

Johnny Morgan

I'll do anything that needs to be done, like emptying the trash and sweeping the place. If you look at some people from diverse ethic groups in Southern California, they're successful at being self-employed because they work hard. They go out and create their own jobs.

Karen McMasters

Somebody that's motivated [will succeed at an online business]. A go-getter. I don't ever stop. I go. I go. I go.

Mike Levinson

… you have to be willing and able to work very hard. You have to be a workaholic. If you're not willing just to work you're not going to succeed.

Rob Yeremian

I'd rather work twelve hours for myself than work eight hours for somebody else.

Mike Ray

I started mowing lawns when I was ten. I started a car detailing business at seventeen and a ticket brokering business for sporting events and concerts when I was in college.

Ray Lindstrom

I always worked and went to school at the same time and I learned a lot about the media.

Starting Your Own Business

Karen McMasters

I'd just say, just go for it! Try it.

Mike Ray

If somebody was really interested I would suggest they go up to their attic or down to their basement and find the most expensive items that they haven't used for the last few years, clean them up, and take some pictures.

Chuck Black

Well, number one, you have to have a decent working knowledge of the computer, especially the Internet.

I would try to find a product that is either not being sold or that only one or two other people are selling.

If you can figure out what trend is coming up, then you can do relatively well.

Bill Cameta

I think that eBay offers incredible opportunity for people to go into business for themselves. You don't have to rent a building, you don't have to hire a staff, and you don't have to advertise.

New equipment is easier to sell and list on eBay because once we create an auction for new equipment we can use it repetitively.

Another thing I want to mention to you, that I think is important, is whatever you're selling, your relationship with your suppliers is crucial.

Brandon Dupsky

To allow a business to be successful you should focus on things that you enjoy, whether it's a product group, a type of service, or a type of item.

... my advice for people selling on eBay: pick a focus, find something you like and run it like a business. You've got to

constantly change; in this environment the competition is at your heels.

Ray Lindstrom

Well, I think the key thing is the product. You've got to have the right product.

You've got to find a product that you can have a ready supply of all the time.

Ravi Sambhwani

The more unique an item you have, the better chance you will have of selling it and succeeding.

Mike Levinson

I'd rather sell ten cars at twenty bucks apiece than maybe stick one guy and sell a car for thirty-five bucks.

Johnny Morgan

Virtually anybody can go out and find a product, turn around and sell it and make a very good living at it.

There are worlds and worlds of opportunity out there. Somebody who's willing to work at it and give better service than the next guy is going to find success.

Martin Mathews

Well, I think it's a great opportunity for everyone. A person can go through the learning curve easily by selling items at first that they don't want or need.

Karen Young

Anybody can do what I did. Anybody can go to an auction or garage sale and buy something for ten dollars and then offer it on eBay for twenty dollars.

Rich Horowitz

I think you just say, "Hey, I can do that!" The interest has to be there first. That is critical to being successful. Again, it's knowing your industry and having interest and passion for it.

Then just say, I think I'm going to try that whether it works or not. I think trying it's the most important thing.

Know your business. Whatever business you're doing, make sure you know it. I think that's the best advice. Don't get involved in something that you don't now anything about.

You try things to see if it works. If it works you keep going along that path. If it doesn't, you change tack.

Rob Yeremian

Well, nobody should start doing eBay full-time right from the start. People should just start doing a few auctions here and there because you can't count on a regular income from eBay.

Start small. Don't get in over your head. You shouldn't partake in any business venture until you know what you're doing.

Mike Wuertz

It's hard to start a business selling on eBay because it is so competitive out there. A lot of the people selling are not business people, and have no idea what their total cost is to sell an item on eBay. You have to figure your listing, your closing, and all your PayPal fees.

The Importance of Honesty

Karen Young

Honestly representing what you are selling is very important. When you're describing the items that you're selling, you have to be honest in your description and mention any flaws the item has. You have to remember that these folks are buying something from you that they've only seen in a two dimensional picture. With your words you have to give them a vision for seeing a three dimensional object.

Rich Horowitz

If it's between grades, use the lower grade. So you track where the prices have gone over the years, and see that it is very, very fairly priced.

Mike Levinson

And the other thing you have to do is you have to be honest to a fault.

Bill Cameta

I try to convey to people what they can expect so they're not disappointed.

The Customer Comes First

Karen Young

The one thing you can do to distinguish yourself from your competition is to offer good customer service.

Even if you know the customer is completely wrong, the customer is still always right. I've kept a lot of that philosophy with me as I've grown my business. I always try to treat my customers as I want to be treated. It's helpful for me to think about what I would want a company to do for me in the same situation. That's what I try to do for my customers.

Bill Cameta

We have a customer service department which we really take seriously. We really take a proactive interest in making sure that the customer's happy.

Rich Horowitz

I think when you are buying something sight unseen, it's important to make people feel comfortable. And so our policy has always been, "If you don't like what you get, send it back."

Our shipping is very fast. When people win something and pay for it, they get it very quickly. The quality is good. I think our overall customer service ensures loyalty.

Ravi Sambhwani

Prompt communication with the customer is important because now everybody wants instant answers.

Mike Ray

The consumers are definitely winning. It's not extremely profitable, but we feel we are building up a great base of customers, who are thrilled with the product that we sell, as well as the service that we provide.

Johnny Morgan

I could make a plastic sign for less money that would save me from spending a lot on raw materials, but I would rather go with the qualities I can give. That's always been my philosophy.

Regard for Employees

Mike Levinson

I have GREAT employees, and this business would not be where it is without their contribution.

Brandon Dupsky

The first intern I hired still works here. I have a lot of people who have worked here for around three or four years. My management team, if you add it up, has about 22 years of experience working with me in a six-year-old company.

Chuck Black

And it's also fun and exciting for me to offer opportunities to my employees. I mean, we have a health insurance plan here, and it's kind of neat.

Rich Horowitz

I started off by myself and eventually got some help. Now my employees are an important part of my business. I give them the flexibility to be creative and come up with their own ideas, which not only benefits me, but it allows them to utilize their individual talents. I trust them explicitly and I believe they trust me.

Working as a Family

Johnny Morgan

My son, Rick, is in the business with me and we both have Master Degrees in Business Administration. He's a computer wiz! He built our website and does most of the computer work with eBay, Yahoo and Amazon.

Karen Young

I've had a lot of help setting up this business from my family. My original website was designed by my brother, and my dad did the programming. My mother is currently my customer service representative. She handles the phones for me.

Ravi Sambhwani

I get a lot of help from my family, from my wife and kids. My son knew everything, so he set me up and posted my items. I started learning from my son. It was with my son's help that I got started.

Martin Mathews

We went from my brother's garage to eventually employing one hundred and thirty-five people.

Having Fun

Karen Young

And the business has always been fun.

Mike Levinson

I tell people that when I go to work, everyday is Christmas. We get stuff delivered, we open those boxes up, and we never know for sure what we're going to get because everyday we get new products. What else could you ask for than to work in a toy store when you're 54 years old!

Chuck Black

To me, it's fun and exciting to make a business successful and figure out new ways to do things.

Ray Lindstrom

I bet you the majority of people are having fun and getting rid of stuff or they're doing it as a hobby. It's so much fun to watch your things go up [for auction] everyday.

Glossary

About Me – An option provided to eBay users that allows them to give visitors information about themselves.

Andale - See Auction Management Service.

Auction Management Service - An assortment of auction support services that assist in managing inventory, listing and scheduling items, re-listing of unsold items, emailing and invoicing winners, and tracking sales data. May include other web hosting services.

AuctionHelper - See Auction Management Service.

AuctionWorks - See Auction Management Service.

Auctiva - See Auction Management Service.

Banner Ads – A small advertising graphic linked to a web page of the advertiser.

BidPay - Secure, online transaction service specialized for auctions. Now known as Western Union auction payments.

Billpoint - An online transaction payment service owned by eBay that was replaced with PayPal when eBay purchased PayPal.

Buy-It-Now (BIN) - eBay auction feature that allows users to buy an item at a set price rather than place a bid and wait for the auction to end.

ChannelAdvisor - See Auction Management Service.

Closing Fee - The Final Value Fee based on the final sale price of the item.

Drop Shipping - Method of shipment where items are sent directly from a supplier's and not the seller's warehouse.

Dutch Auction - An auction for more than one of the same item where a buyer may bid on one or up to all of the items.

eBay Drop-off - A term used to describe an independent business where customers can bring in items to be photographed, described, and listed for auction on eBay. When the items are sold the business retains a commission and the customer is paid the remainder of the net proceeds from the sale. Usually the items are left on consignment.

eBay Live - A special annual convention held by eBay which includes seminars, guest speakers and workshops. It is an event where eBay users can network with each other.

eBay Store - An eBay store allows eBay sellers to show all of their items. It also provides a way for them to give more information about themselves and their business. It enables sellers to customize their web pages to project individuality and personality.

Epinions.com - A comparison shopping website owned by shopping.com.

Gallery Photo - An optional photo displayed next to the title of an item listed by an eBay seller.

Google - World Wide Web search engine which employs a unique and patented system. Google ranks every web page by how many other web pages link back to it. A system like this ensures that searches return the most relevant results from the smallest amount of information.

HTML - Stands for HyperText Markup Language. It is a programming or coding language used to create web pages.

Insertion Fee - A term used on eBay to describe the fee based on the starting price or the fixed item price of items offered for auction. As the price increases the insertion fee increases.

JPEG - Stands for Joint Photographic Experts Group format which compresses graphics and photographic color depth making them smaller and quicker to download.

Listing Fee - A fee based on the starting price of an item or the reserve price if there is one. This term is usually used to describe a Yahoo auction pricing fee, but is sometimes used to refer to the Insertion Fee on eBay auctions.

Glossary

Merchant Account - An account which allows a merchant to accept credit card transactions.

Microsoft Access - A program to create and manage databases.

Omidyar, Pierre - eBay founder.

Overture - A search engine service that allows a customer to pay for search results based on popular words or phrases which are specific to their business.

Paymentech - See Merchant Account.

PayPal - Secure, online transaction service popular with eBay users. PayPal's basic service allows users to send or receive money. These transactions can be made utilizing their bank account or credit card.

Pay-per-click - An agreement that allows a merchant to only pay for traffic based on the number of clicks to his site.

PowerSeller - A term given to qualified eBay sellers who maintain a required sales volume. The seller must also meet the requirement of a specified positive feedback rating.

PriceGrabber.com - A comparison shopping website.

Reserve - See Reserve Price.

Reserve Price - The lowest price a seller is willing to accept for an item. Items with a reserve price will not be sold unless the set minimum price is met. Sometimes referred to as "Reserve."

Seller's Assistant Pro - A sales management tool offered by eBay.

Sell-through Rate - Percentage of visitors who actually purchase an item when clicking through to a merchant's website.

Server - A computer which provides a service to an end user typically over an Internet connection, such as a web server which "serves" web requests to a user who is browsing the web.

Shopping.com - A comparison shopping website.

Spam - Unsolicited email.

Turbo Lister - A listing tool offered by eBay.

Vendio - See Auction Management Service.

Whitman, Meg - eBay CEO.

Yahoo - One of the first World Wide Web search engines. Yahoo has expanded their business to include services such as directory guides, e-commerce, web hosting, and career services. Their core business remains their search engine technology.

Yahoo Store - A program provided by Yahoo that allows the user to create a web based online store. It offers a variety of options which provides a turnkey approach to setting up an attractive commercial website and includes all the features that a merchant will require.

Index

Index